Behind the Badge

By Ewart "Gus" Wersch, Chief RTD.

A History of Policing in Carleton County
from 1909 to 1988

~

Acknowledgements

Special appreciation to Roxane Healey and her immediate support staff at Motion Creative Printing for their friendly guidance in the development of this publication.

Special thanks to Michael Raganold of WICMS.com for his encouragement and support to bring this publication to its completion.

Thanks to the staff at the Nepean Museum for their tireless effort in developing the Nepean Police Display for your viewing pleasure.

A special thanks to all the Nepean Police staff that served with me over the many years with their contributions to this publication, through the photographs and text.

A special thanks to the Nepean Police Identification Branch, Staff Sgt. Brian McGarvey and Sgt. Wayne Levere for the many photographs used in this publication.

Thanks to Staff Sgt. Ron Driscoll for his contribution whenever a vital information question needed an answer.

Special thanks to Pauline and Ron Meyer for their editing support.

Table of Contents

Behind the Badge

PART ONE

ONTARIO PROVINCIAL POLICE

~ CHAPTER 1 ~

Ontario Provincial Police History Background: 1909–1949

A Brief History of the Ontario Provincial Police

"Proud to Serve"

On October 13, 1909, a provincial Order-in-Council decreed the establishment of the "Ontario Provincial Police Force" – a permanent force of salaried police constables. From its earliest days to today, the strength of the O.P.P. has been its people.

The O.P.P.'s roots can be traced back to the 19th century. John Wilson Murray, the province's first full-time paid criminal detective, began his 31-year career in 1875. A small staff of government detectives worked for the Attorney General's office up until 1909. At the time of the O.P.P.'s formation, many of the individuals already working directly for the province as "provincial constables" were subsequently hired by the O.P.P.

John Wilson Murray
Ontario's First "Provincial
Constable"

The O.P.P.'s first chief of police, Superintendent Joseph E. Rogers, commanded six inspectors and 38 constables. During these early years, many officers worked in one-person detachments with no radio communication or motor vehicle transportation.

In the early 1920s, the successive appointments of two military men to the position of commissioner helped transform the organization. Badge numbers, military style uniforms, insignia, and protocols all helped define the character of the new and expanding force.

In 1930, motorcycle personnel from the Department of Public Highways joined the O.P.P. motorcycle patrol to police Ontario's increasingly busy highways. In 1941, the O.P.P. made a major purchase of marked cruisers – the beginning of an indelible link of cruiser and patrol officer. The war years also saw the formation of volunteer groups who assisted officers with their duties. These were the forebears of today's O.P.P. Auxiliary Program.

The introduction of a radio system in 1947 (considered at the time to be the largest, most modern police communication system of its kind) heralded a new era in communications. The 1950s saw an increase in the volume of vehicles on roads, and in 1956, 75 percent of members were busy enforcing the Highway Traffic Act. Shortly thereafter, the O.P.P. began using underwater breathing equipment for the first time and snow vehicles in the north.

A major reorganization of the O.P.P., initiated by Commissioner Eric Silk, characterized the 1960s. What followed was a period of rapid growth through modernization, diversity and training. For example, in 1965 the O.P.P. became the first Canadian police service to commence traffic law enforcement by air.

Excerpted from http://www.opp.ca/Community/Museum/opp_001071.html

Stan Batt and Alf Andrews in front of one of the first patrol cars, a 1941 Chevrolet coupe.

With the introduction of the new fleet of cars, the motorcycles were saved for narrow stretches and congested areas where the officers could weave through traffic to the accident scene.

Fifteen of the cars were divided into three districts and assigned to patrol the new QEW Highway. Other cars were used in strategic spots, Northern Ontario and on other main highways.

The QEW Highway as it was in 1939. The photo was taken near Clarkson Road (Erin Mills Parkway).

All bundled up for the cold (from left): Alf Andrews, Stan Batt, W.E. Herman, Jack Hinchcliffe, F. Bell and Cecil Bean.

Excerpted from REVIEW December 1986

Motorcycle officers Stan Batt and Donald Pickell on Lakeshore Boulevard in Mimico in 1937.

Memories

By Jeff Wilks, Humber College Student

The Golden Helmets are probably happy that times have changed since 1937. In 1937, officers supplied their motorcycles which today would cost them $14,000 each.

About 75 motorcycles are in use now – not many more than in 1937 when 40 or 50 bikes patrolled the road – however, it was not uncommon 50 years ago for several of those men to be off work because of accidents.

Motorcycles dominated patrolling of the highways. In fact, it wasn't until 1941 that the first Chevrolet coupes were introduced. The first five of these carried stretchers for emergencies. The rest were equipped with a crowbar, a fireman's axe, shovel, tow rope, fire extinguisher and a complete first aid kit.

"Emergency screeching" was provided by a siren on the car's exhaust, and a "police" light was used at night. There were no radar guns, just the dependability of the officer's speedometer for catching speeders.

Excerpted from REVIEW December 1986

Yesterday

Immediately following confederation, a limited number of police were established throughout the province. On the whole, these officers were untrained and unpaid; any remuneration they may have received for their services was derived through the fee system. Their services were limited and their authority was confined to the county, district, city or town in which they were serving.

In 1875, the necessity for giving certain constables jurisdiction throughout the province was recognized. This consideration resulted in the appointment in July of that year of John Wilson Murray to act as a

John Wilson Murray
Ontario's First "Provincial Constable"

"Detective for the province of Ontario" to pursue criminals and run them down in their havens of refuge wherever they may be. Murray performed his varied duties under the direction of Sir Oliver Mowat, the Attorney General of the province for 31 years, travelling to many parts of the world in the apprehension of persons wanted for crimes in Ontario. Following the appointment of John Murray, a major reform occurred when, under the "Constables Act" (R.S.O. 1877), province wide authority was granted to provincial constables appointed by county judges in every county and district throughout Ontario.

Later, the opening up of the mining areas in the north of the province and the accompanying lawlessness, brought to the government the realization that more adequate law enforcement measures were a necessity. Consequently, an Order-in-Council dated October 13, 1909 (confirmed by 10 Edv. VII, c. 39) was passed providing for the establishment of the "Ontario Provincial Police Force", composed of 45 members including the Superintendent and such inspectors as were deemed necessary. The officers were stationed throughout the northern portion of the province and at all border points in southern Ontario. The force was completely reorganized in 1921 under the authority of The Ontario Police Act; a new commanding officer was appointed with the title of Commissioner (Commissioner of Police for Ontario) and the strength of the Force increased to 195.

The Constables Act was amended in 1929 with a view to establishing a closer relationship and cooperation between the Provincial Police Force and County Constabularies. Twenty-eight counties took advantage of this legislation and a member of the Ontario Provincial Police was appointed as acting high constable in each County.

In March 1930, the control and administration of the highway patrolmen, who had been enforcing the Highway Traffic Act under the supervision of the Department of Public Highways, was transferred to the Department of the Attorney General under the Commissioner of Police for Ontario (O.P.P.).

By the Police Act, 1946, proclaimed February 1, 1947, all former legislation dealing with constables was repealed and the duties and responsibilities of police forces were clearly defined for the first time in the history of the province.

Source unknown

MAJOR STEP FORWARD
WAS IN COMMUNICATIONS

Until 1947, officers on patrol duty were limited by telephone communication to their assigned detachment office from locations within their patrol zone.

As an example, an officer patrolling Highway 17 west through Carp when a serious motor vehicle collision would occur just east of Carp behind him. A telephone call would be made to the Ottawa detachment from the collision scene for assistance, but the patrol car now in Kinburn a few miles west of Carp could not be contacted until the officer stopped at a gasoline station and call the detachment by telephone to see if any calls for service had been received for his patrol area.

This changed when on November 27th, 1947, a Radio Communications System was installed under the supervision of Professor J.E. Reid of the University of Toronto. The call for service could now be forwarded to the patrol officer by radio as soon as the dispatcher received the call from the scene by telephone.

Three fixed Stations were installed at Aurora, Whitby and Brampton, with receiving radios in 50 patrol cars. This was a major communication step forward as it was called, "Speed of Light Communications Aids in Catching Law Breakers".

By 1950 there were 50 fixed Stations and 368 Radio equipped vehicles in the field.

Five repeating stations were installed which completed a province wide network. A few years later walkie-talkies were introduced for use by constables on foot, each weighing eight and a half pounds.

The central control room was located in Toronto connected by wire to a high elevation site in Aurora Ontario.

In 1949 when I arrived in Ottawa for my first posting, the patrol cars were radio equipped, and I remember that a half hour was set aside each day to receive special transmissions originating from Toronto. The messages were being relayed from fixed stations across Ontario to the local detachments and to the patrol cars. All stolen vehicle license plate numbers and wanted criminals, such as escapees, etc. were priority items of information to the field officers on patrol in Ontario.

The patrol officer would pull off the highway and copy all the messages. I know from personal experience that on a number of occasions while myself and other patrol officers were receiving these transmissions an actual stolen vehicle would be passing by and be apprehended......the electronic age had arrived.

~ CHAPTER 2 ~

Carleton County Police and Ontario Provincial Police 1929–1938

Carleton County Police Force 1929
Charles McCarthy, W. Hall, B. Conley, Harry Snider

The Carleton County Police Force in 1929 consisted of four officers, Chief Charles McCarthy, Cst. Borden Conley, Cst. W. Hall and Cst. Harry Snider. The three constables used motorcycles for general patrol of Carleton County, which included the ten Townships bordering the City of Ottawa.

In 1938 the force was abolished. Activity background and reports are not available as records were not preserved. Gloucester Township seemed to have a greater involvement with the Carleton County Police and other staff.

Cst. Borden Conley was promoted to Sgt., in 1933, and when the force was abolished he was appointed a By-Law enforcement officer for Nepean Township in May 1938. Chief McCarthy also became a By-Law enforcement officer for the Township of Gloucester. Cst. Harry Snider became the Fire Department Chief for the Township of Nepean. Cst. W. Hall was involved in a motor vehicle accident and passed away.

This ended the era of the Carleton County Police Force in Nepean Township as the Provincial Police took over the general police duties of Carleton County along with their regular patrol of the provincial highways through Carleton County leading to Ottawa, the capital of Canada.

~ CHAPTER 3 ~

Nepean Township Police Established For Northern Part Of Nepean: Westboro-Nepean Township Police 1945–1950

Westboro was that part of the Township of Nepean from Island Park Drive in the East to Carling Avenue in the South, the Ottawa River to the North and West to Britannia area with the Richmond Road being the major thorough fare.

Westboro was the fastest growing town in Ontario and had been declared a Police Village. When a Municipality reaches a population of five thousand in Ontario it is required to establish its own Police service. Westboro established its own police service in 1945 with Borden Conley being appointed Chief of Police for the Westboro-Nepean Township Police.

Chief of Police Borden Conley

Westboro-Nepean Township Police Department 1945–1950 Chief Borden Conley front row fourth from left

The Westboro-Nepean Township Police building was located near the Richmond Road on Churchill Avenue and became a focal point for the area.

The next change in the Police service to Nepean occurred on Jan 1ˢᵗ, 1950 as the City of Ottawa annexed all of Westboro and some additional territory of Nepean Township leaving the remainder of Nepean with a population of approximately 2,200 residents.

OTTAWA CITY POLICE (Next Policing Change)

When Westboro was annexed by Ottawa Jan 1ˢᵗ, 1950, all police officers were absorbed into the Ottawa City Police if they so desired. Ottawa extended its city boundaries to include the area between Carling Avenue to the south along Baseline Road and as far west as # 7 highway.

ONTARIO PROVINCIAL POLICE

While all these changes were taking place, the remainder of Nepean Township and Carleton County were served by the Ontario Provincial Police. From 1929 to 1938 the Ontario Provincial Police were involved with motorcycle patrols of the provincial highways running through Carleton County and gave assistance in serious criminal cases to the four man Carleton County Police Force. The Provincial Police took over the full responsibility of the police services in Carleton County as the Carleton County Police were dissolved in 1938. As of 1941 the Provincial Police used the first patrol cars for general police duties.

Photo of one of the first Patrol cars in 1941.

* **More Police changes were in the offing for Carleton County in 1957.**

Due to the rapid population increase in the suburban areas of Nepean and Gloucester Townships, the Province of Ontario advised the two Townships that they had exceeded the 5,000 population level and were required to establish their own police services.

~ CHAPTER 4 ~

Gloucester-Nepean Township Police
1957–1964

O n July 1ˢᵗ, 1957 a joint Gloucester-Nepean Township Police service was established to provide the police services for the two municipalities.

John Rankin was appointed Chief of Police to head the new police force. Geographically, the joint police service had problems, as the Rideau River divided the two townships; without bridges over the Rideau River, this created serious problems to effectively co-ordinate patrols and respond to major occurrences in emergencies. Another major issue was the cost sharing; as Nepean was growing at a faster rate, it required more calls for service, staff and equipment.

By the fall of 1963 the two municipalities agreed to dissolve the joint police service and establish their own police departments to take effect on January 1ˢᵗ, 1964.

The following pages present the By-Laws that were required to give legal authorization to the changes.

By-Law 21-57 Authorization to establish the joint Gloucester-Nepean Township Police.

By-Law 72-63 Authorization to abolish the joint Gloucester-Nepean Township Police.

BY-LAWS:

BY-LAW NUMBER 21-57

BEING a By-Law to establish a Municipal Police Force for the Township of Nepean and the Township of Gloucester and to authorize an agreement for the management and operation of said Police Force.

WHEREAS it is deemed advisable to establish a Municipal Police Force for the Township of Nepean and the Township of Gloucester pursuant to Sub-section 5 of Section 386 of the Municipal Act Chapter 243, R.S.O. 1950 as amended.

NOW THEREFORE, the Council of the Municipal Corporation of the Township of Nepean enacts as follows:-

THAT the Reeve and Clerk be and they are hereby authorized to sign an agreement with the Township of Gloucester to establish a Municipal Police Force for the Township of Nepean and the Township of Gloucester and to provide for the management and operation of said Police Force.

PASSED and given under the Hands of the Reeve and Clerk and the Corporate Seal of the Municipal Corporation of the Township of Nepean this 13th day of June 1957.

Andrew MacLean	D.A. Moodie
Clerk	Reeve

THE ABOVE IS A COPY OF THE ORIGINAL BY-LAW

CORPORATION OF THE TOWNSHIP OF NEPEAN

By-Law No. 72-63

Being a By-Law to dissolve the Municipal
Police Force established under By-Law No.
21-57 of the Corporation of the Township
of Nepean and By-Law No. 35 of 1957 of the
Corporation of the Township of Gloucester.

— — — — — — —

WHEREAS it is deemed advisable to dissolve the
Municipal Police Force for the Township of Nepean and the
Township of Gloucester which was established pursuant to
Sub-section 5 of Section 386 of The Municipal Act, Chapter
243, R.S.O. 1950 as amended.

NOW THEREFORE, the Council of the Municipal
Corporation of the Township of Nepean enacts as follows:

That By-Law No. 21-57 of the Corporation of
the Township of Nepean, passed on the 13th
day of June, 1957, be and is hereby rescinded
and repealed to be effective on the 31st day
of December, 1963.

That the agreement made on the 1st day of
November, 1957 between The Corporation of the
Township of Gloucester and The Corporation of
the Township of Nepean be considered null and
void as of the 31st day of December, 1963.

PASSED AND GIVEN under the Hands of the Reeve
and Clerk and the Corporate Seal of the Municipal Corporation
of the Township of Nepean this 28th day of November, 1963.

_____
Reeve

_____
Clerk

THE ABOVE IS A COPY OF THE ORIGINAL BY-LAW

Behind the Badge

PART TWO

Preface

Life rewards are reaped from our involvement with the people around us in the community we serve. I had this privilege to serve the residents of Carleton County in general and Nepean in particular as a police officer from 1949 to my retirement on May 31st, 1988. The legacy we leave behind us is not what we did, but how we made an impact in the community by fulfilling the mandate we were given.

Every person deserves respect and consideration in how we resolve issues that require our attention. We are here for a moment of time and it's how we do our jobs during this time that we earn the trust of the residents who for various reasons have difficult situations to deal with and need our guidance and support, especially in the many instances where life and death is an issue.

The stories you will read, in some cases, left an impact on the lives of some residents who erred in their ways.

By applying restitution rather than prosecution, we turned many lives around and helped those with problems to establish themselves as good productive citizens in our communities, like the seven high school students replacing the damage they had done rather than being charged with a criminal record, or the gentleman who approached me years later to state that the chance for making restitution gave him the opportunity to turn his life around and become one of the largest construction company owners in the area.

Or, the trust you establish with the likes of four young men who were out on the town on New Year`s Eve in a jeep, and as I had just completed my tour of duty and booked in at my residence, they decided to park on the sidewalk at the Manotick Tea Room under my window singing Christmas Carols for my benefit in the freezing weather. This was earned respect in reverse.

Let`s start our journey....come walk with me for a mile, or two, or three....in my shoes...

Ewart Gus Wersch, Chief of Police for Nepean, retired.

~ CHAPTER 5 ~

The Policing Of Carleton County By The Ontario Provincial Police: 1949–1964

The Ontario Provincial Police were responsible for policing the remainder of Nepean Township after the annexation of Westboro by the City of Ottawa, including the other nine Townships in Carleton County, from their detachment at 1663 Bank Street until July 1st, 1957.

From July 1957 the Provincial Police no longer provided direct police service to the Townships of Gloucester and Nepean. These two municipalities had established a joint Police Service which continued to January 1st 1964. They then abolished the joint police service and established their own separate Police services, continuing to police their own municipalities from 1964 to January 1st,1994.

The Ontario Provincial Police continued to police the remaining eight Townships until January 1st, 1994.

Note: On January 1st, 1994 the City of Ottawa amalgamated the total Carleton County Police Service including Nepean and Gloucester Townships

ONTARIO PROVINCIAL POLICE: 1949–1964

Policing Carleton County other than Gloucester and Nepean Townships.

The following is a separate account of the police service in Carleton County as it relates to the Ontario Provincial Police from 1949 –1964.

It was on December 19th, 1949 that I (Ewart Gus Wersch) arrived at the Ottawa Detachment to start my police career. I can give a personal account of the police service from a hands on point of view until Jan 12th, 1964. Some major investigations are reported in this segment.

The OPP-Ottawa Detachment had been established at 1663 Bank Street in 1946 to serve all of Carleton County until July 1st,1957. Rockliffe Park within the City of Ottawa was policed by one officer under the jurisdiction of the Ottawa Provincial Police Detachment.

The Ontario Provincial Police Detachments in Ontario, related to the court jurisdictions within their area of responsibility. In this case the Carleton County Court house located on Nicholas Street in Ottawa was the location where all cases that occurred in Carleton County were heard.

The Ottawa Detachment Staff as of September 30th, 1946
Back Row: Cst. C.B. Cresswell, Sgt. Stringer, Cst. Frank Patterson
Front Row: Cst. Geo. Hobbs, Cst. Chris Doherty, Cst. A.L. Robertson, Cst. Keith McLaren

~ CHAPTER 6 ~

Ontario Provincial Police — Personal Hands-On Service: 1949–1964

My career as a police officer starts here on November 1st, 1949 and ends with my retirement on May 31st, 1988.

After applying to the Ontario Provincial Police in October, 1949, I was accepted and directed to report to the Ontario Police College at Ajax, Ontario by midnight October 31st, 1949 to start a seven week Basic Police Training Course, which cov-

Ontario Provincial Police Ottawa Attachment
1663 Bank Street, Ottawa, 1953

ered, police procedures, federal and provincial laws, court procedures, self defence and firearms' training, as well as report writing.

The Ontario Provincial Police College at Ajax was part of the former Air Force training base used during the war which consisted mainly of classrooms and temporary living quarters. The College was later relocated to Aylmer, Ontario and served as the Ontario Police College to house and train municipal police recruits.

On December 16th, 1949, the training course was completed, all graduates were assigned to various districts throughout Ontario.

One of the temporary Police College buildings

I was assigned to #11 District Headquarters in Cornwall Ontario, arriving on December 19th, 1949. After orientation to the area, I was sent to the Ottawa Detachment, located in Ottawa at 1663 Bank Street.

The province was divided into 17 Ontario Provincial Police Districts, which had a number of operational detachments within each district.

The Ottawa Detachment was located at 1663 Bank St., Ottawa and all the police service for Carleton County, which included ten townships, was provided from this office.

Sgt Jack Hinchcliffe – Officer in charge of the Ottawa Detachment in 1949

A Detachment Commander, Sergeant Jack Hinchliffe was responsible to the District Headquarters Inspector, in Cornwall Ontario; the District Headquarters Inspector was accountable to the Ontario Provincial Police General Headquarters located at Toronto, Ontario.

The officer in charge of the Provincial Police held the Rank of Commissioner.

Staff Sgt. John Hinchliffe passed away at the age of 58 years after serving 28 years in the OPP in the Toronto and Ottawa area. I was asked to be a pall bearer at his funeral service.

Constable Jack Hinchliffe shown in the above photo in civilian clothes was one of the original 80 officers assigned to the motorcycle patrol in 1930. The 1931 Henderson KJ motorcycle is the oldest OPP vehicle in the Museum's collection, it was first owned by Constable John Hinchliffe.

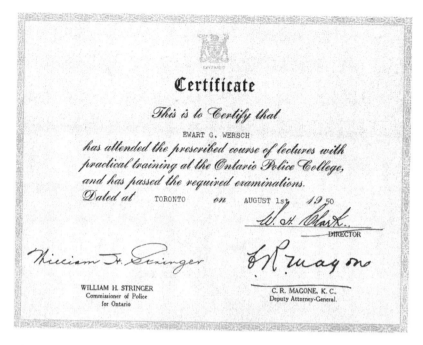

Certificate

This is to Certify that

EWART G. WERSCH

has attended the prescribed course of lectures with practical training at the Ontario Police College, and has passed the required examinations.

Dated at TORONTO on AUGUST 1st 19 50

W. H. Clark
DIRECTOR

William H. Stringer

WILLIAM H. STRINGER
Commissioner of Police
for Ontario

C. R. MAGONE, K. C.
Deputy Attorney-General.

After the initial orientation at District Headquarters I proceeded to Ottawa arriving at the Ottawa Detachment on Dec 20th, 1949. This became the starting point of my operational Police career for the next 15 years.

Carleton County is the area that borders the City of Ottawa on three sides, with the northern boundary being the Ottawa River which is also the boundary between Ontario and Quebec.

The major highways that enter Ottawa must come through Carleton County, such as the Trans Canada #17 east and west, #15 Highway to the south west towards Toronto, #16 Highway straight south from Ottawa which joins Highway #401 or Old #2 highway at Prescott and to the United States international-al border, and # 31 Highway which goes slightly south-east to Morrisburg, again ending at #2 or #401 highways, which head east to Montreal, Quebec and west to Toronto.

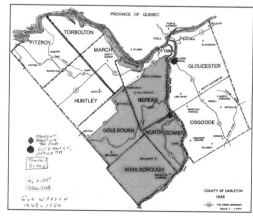

Shaded area reflects my first patrol zone Dec 20th, 1949 to December 1953 while stationed at Manotick

---

The staff at the Ottawa Detachment, consisted of a Sergeant, the officer in charge, two Corporals, in charge of field operations Criminal and Traffic, five Patrol officers, with a civilian person for secretarial duties.

With five major highways going through our jurisdiction to the Capital of Canada, traffic was exceptionally heavy, not only to service Ottawa, but also a major crossing point to western Quebec. With only five field officers available it would be impossible to cover the area on a twenty four hour, seven day week basis.

Simple arithmetic for a five eight hour per day shift, covering a seven day period twenty-four hours per day, equals 21 eight hour shifts. This requires four and one-fifth officers to field one officer for the area on a twenty-four hour basis.

With only five officers available, each requiring at least one day off per week, to cover court appearances, sick leave or annual vacation it meant that the shifts were scheduled to mainly cover the day and afternoon period. Officers were on call during the night, every night, mainly for traffic collisions.

On arrival at the Ottawa Detachment and after a short orientation by the officer in charge I was assigned a Patrol area in Carleton County to start my first shift on December 21st, 1949 a few days before Christmas.

The area I was assigned bordered on the east side by the Rideau River and #16 highway, the West side by #15 highway and the north by the City of Ottawa. The area covered four townships which had seven small villages within these boundaries.

It was a hectic introduction into the real world of police work, never having any field experience, it was like being thrown to the wolves. This was no ordinary job where you had time to work into the day to day operations of a company, you were out there dealing with tragedies, serious traffic collisions, injuries, criminal activity, etc., from your very first shift. All you had to fall back on was the seven weeks of intense Police College instructions.

The following is a summary of what occurred in the first ten days of my life as a patrol officer. On the late afternoon of December 20th, I drove to Manotick about 10 miles south of Ottawa on #16 highway which was more or less the central point of my patrol area. The Manotick Tea Room was a small restaurant with rooms to rent, it had been pre-arranged that I room at this location and work in all directions from this location.

The Corporal (Carl Johns) drove out to Manotick about eleven o'clock on December 21st, 1949, and took me on an introductory tour of the area with my first Patrol Car #1129 until about three p.m., then we headed back to the detachment office in Ottawa where he got out and said "you're on your own".

My main assignment was to patrol the two provincial highways, #16 and #15, as these were the routes where the heavy transportation fed into Ottawa from # 401 highway, the USA, and Toronto.

All the other calls for service and complaints within the area were covered on a call by call basis. I worked about sixteen hours per day for the first week, driving into every town and covered all the side roads to make sure I knew the area in case of emergency calls.

My shift schedule was as follows:

> On Patrol: 10 a.m. to 12 noon
> Off for lunch and report writing: 12 noon to 2 p.m.
> On Patrol: 2 p.m. to 6 p.m.
> Off for supper and report completion: 6 p.m. to 8 p.m.
> On Patrol: 8 p.m. to 10.00 p.m.

This schedule was based on a six day work week with Sundays off but on call for traffic collisions and other emergencies 24 hours per day.

The schedule actually married me to the job – where could you go before 10 a.m. or after 10 p.m.? On my day off I had to report to the detachment officer and leave my telephone number so I could be contacted in case of emergencies in my patrol zone. If serious, other officers would take over, if they were available, until I went home to Manotick to pick up my equipment and the patrol car and drive to the scene of the incident.

The basic starting salary was $1,940.00 per year which included a free uniform, a six day working week, no overtime. Because we worked a six day week with no overtime, we were given the traditional three weeks annual leave, with an extra week to cover all the callbacks and the extra sixth shift per week as compared to other five day per week jobs.

It was fortunate that the first few days were quiet days, only a few minor traffic collisions and thefts, which allowed me to get more in tune with the area.

We were fast approaching the holiday season and as expected drinking and driving was the same old problem and it didn't take long to be introduced to this combination.

While on patrol I overtook a vehicle that was crossing the centre line a number of times indicating that this could be an impaired driver. When I pulled alongside the driver took off but unfortunately he only went about a half mile when he drove off the highway into a snow bank. I had everything you could imagine, teenagers under the influence and a regular liquor store, beer, wine and several brands of whisky.

Provincial Police Constable Ewart Gus Wersch First Patrol car # 1129, note high neck tunic still in use. December 21st, 1949

They were from the Manotick area and with the buzz around that a new police officer was in town, it didn't take long that the word was out about the tough police officer who didn't tolerate this type of activity.

In a way it was a good introduction, I didn't have a problem and gained respect in a hurry, especially from the older folk.

A Not So Merry Christmas Dec 24th,1949

Just outside the Ottawa City limits on Christmas Eve, a bread truck was delivering bread to homes, the truck was parked well off the shoulder of #16 highway.

A teenager who was helping the bread delivery man to make some extra money, was loading his carrying basket at the rear of the truck when a drunken driver drove into the back of the truck jamming the youth between the vehicle bumpers.

Unfortunately the youth lost one leg which ended his career as a hockey player.

A Not So Lucky Holiday Trip. Dec 25th, 1949

On Christmas morning I came along the highway a few miles from Manotick and saw some fresh car tracks and broken guard rails on the right side of the road. On checking, I saw a vehicle upside down in a gully with the driver pinned under the car soaked in gasoline.

It was a dangerous situation until we were able to lift the car and free the driver, who wasn't seriously injured, however, because he was lying pinned under the car in gasoline with his clothes on, this actually caused the gasoline to scald the skin on his back.

We can wash our hands in gasoline to remove grease or paint and it won't burn as long as its done in the open air, as soon as a wet gasoline soaked cloth is wrapped around your skin for a few minutes it will react and become a serious burn injury.

The driver's back was totally scalded and he spent the next four months in hospital which was a painful ordeal for him, receiving many skin grafts.

The driver apparently fell asleep, alcohol was not involved in this instance.

During my first ten day period I investigated about 20 collisions, and by this time had a number of court cases pending. It was a quick introduction to hands on police work.

"Due to the many changes in the police service from 1929 to 1964, some duplication may have taken place in this document, however, it was necessary to show how the police services were entwined or embedded with each other".

I stayed in Manotick until the fall of 1953, working in the area, and was well established taking part in community activities such as hockey and baseball, playing on the local Manotick baseball team.

During our introduction at the police college we were advised to become involved in the community where we were posted, especially with the youth. The director at the police college did not mention that if we were injured in any activity other than related to our official duties, we would not be eligible for compensation

In June of 1951 while playing baseball for the Manotick team, upon sliding into home plate I unfortunately fractured my left wrist, which put me off work for nine weeks.

Although I was involved in promoting good relations with the community, it was not accepted as a compensation case in those days, it cost me four weeks holidays, plus all my sick leave and still I was off without pay for three weeks.

The Manotick ball team and the area communities held a benefit ball game and raised enough money to pay for my doctor's medical bill which came to one hundred and ten dollars.

JOHN BRACKEN MAKES IT OFFICIAL—Although Manotick won the championship of the South Carleton Softball League last Friday, the triumph wasn't official until last night when John Bracken presented Manotick captain Mike Kelly with the Bracken Shield. Manotick retained the shield for the second straight year by downing Osgoode Little Chiefs four games to three in a best-of-seven series. Members of the winning team pictured above are, back row: left to right, Ron Watson, Ed Reilly, Carl Saunders, Gus Wersch, Joe Bulger, Fred Nicholls and Don Driscoll. Front row, left to right: Phil Kelly, Gord Hardy, John Bracken, Mike Kelly, Fred Pay, Linus Kelly and Karl Wilson. Missing when the picture was taken were Art Scobie and Cliff Walker.

I continued to involve myself in sports activities in the Manotick area, working with the local teenagers and business leaders of the day as it was the thing to do.

While stationed at Manotick, I followed the motto, to work with the people for the people, which earned respect for the police force and ultimately myself. There are many stories to tell, some are humorous but had an effect on the recipients.

Foolish Halloween Prank

Some teenagers let the air out of a local doctor's car tires which was parked in his driveway. It so happened I caught them in the act. Instead of charging them with mischief, and since I had the keys to the local garage where I stored the patrol car, I made them get the wheeled car jack from the garage, lift the car removing the wheels, rolling them to the garage a few blocks away, and returning them filled with air.

This took about an hour under the supervision of the Doctor and myself. They all received a lecture about the Doctor being immobilized in case he was called for an emergency. The feedback from the locals was beyond belief; apparently, officers who had served in the area before I came did not get involved and gave the pretense that they were better than the people they served.

Another Interesting Halloween Case

One Halloween night, problems occurred with a gang of six teenagers in the Kars area. These young adults drove along the side roads in the farming community causing damage to the farmers' fields, farm machinery, and dumping stacked hay bales.

Answering the call, it didn't take long to find the car parked on a side road, as I shone my spot light into the field I could see them going from hay bale to hay bale, shouting and gesturing. It was a cat and mouse game in which I couldn't win until I got the idea to immobilize their transportation as they were miles from nowhere. While keeping the spotlight on them in the field I lifted the hood, took the distributor cap off, removed the rotor, replaced the cap, closed the hood and drove away with the rotor in my pocket. I patrolled the general area without receiving any complaints for the rest of the night from the farming community.

At six in the morning I returned to the car; it had frost on the windows and, of course, couldn't be started without the rotor. I would have given anything to hear and see them try to start the car. I replaced the rotor and heard later that they couldn't figure out what I done to their car so it wouldn't start, yet when they came to pick it up with a tow truck around eight a.m. it started just fine.

Train Collision at Ashton

On Friday March 18th, 1950 just a few months after I started on the job I received a call at my residence to go to Ashton train siding area. Across country side roads from Manotick it would be about twenty-five miles, however, due to a severe snowstorm traffic was at a standstill.

Instead of going the short route I headed north to Ottawa on #16 highway, then west to Highway #15 highway, which headed southwest to Ashton. The train accident occurred at 1:10 A.M. and due to the road conditions I arrived at 3:15 A.M. which normally would have been a 25 minute trip.

The Ashton Train Station had a long rail siding and was a central meeting place for the trains to meet and pass. Due to the storm the freight train going east with a long row of box cars was behind schedule and didn't clear the mainline. The west bound freight train was on time and was not aware that about 15 or so box cars were still on the mainline.

The collision threw the west bound engine off the track into the north ditch facing east, a huge number of box cars were demolished. I can still see the fireman sitting in the cab of the engine, with a yellowish complexion, the steam lines had broken from the impact and literally steam cooked him, the engineer was thrown clear but did not survive.

One of the demolished box cars was loaded with cartons of Bata shoes. They were all over the place and even in this weather people came out from the area and started to loot the shoes and other goods strewn about.

1950 Airplane Crash of Note

United States Ambassador Steinhart to Canada was returning to his office and residence in Ottawa from a trip. The airplane was approaching from the east when the motor stalled and it crashed with the Ambassador, pilot and one other passenger being killed. I received a call the next day to be the security guard at the gated entrance to the residence in Rockliffe Park for dignitaries entering the premises. This is when I met Lester Pearson who at that time was in charge of protocol for the external affairs, later to become Prime Minister of Canada.

Ambulance Call Out Policy

The policy of the Ambulance service were not to leave Ottawa if called by anyone other than the Police, had been in force in the area because too many calls were made for minor cuts and bruises. This created extra pressure on myself and other patrol officers when we received a call that a serious vehicle collision had occurred with injuries. Often we would be thirty miles away, and had to get to the scene before the ambulance would leave Ottawa. We had to drive as quickly as possible with our emergency lights and siren blowing, the adrenaline would be at an all time high.

The motorists who stopped at the scene anxiously awaited the arrival of the patrol car and, as you crested the last hill before the scene, those at the scene felt that immediate aid had arrived, we were looked upon as a demi-God. We had our first aid kit and basic training, but it was a frustrating situation as the ambulance wait time had endangered the lives of injured motorists. This was corrected when additional ambulances were made available, as well as being located in different areas supported by the Fire Department Emergency vehicles in the area communities.

Cattle Rustling Cases

A report was received from a farmer in Torbolton Township that one of his animals was missing from the pasture on his farm. A person who was living in the area was a prime suspect from previous investigations. As I entered the laneway leading to the suspect's residence and out buildings, a pickup truck was leaving in a hurry.

The first thing I noticed was a rope and block and tackle near the entrance to the residence which had red blood stains that looked fresh. On questioning the suspect, he stated that if I wanted to look any further, I would need a search warrant. I told the suspect that another patrol car was bringing a search arrant and that I would remain in the suspect's yard until the warrant was delivered.

As soon as the warrant to search was delivered, a search behind the shed in a wooded area was conducted and at the base of a tree we found the remains of a freshly butchered animal as described by the farmer who reported the loss.

The suspect was arrested and admitted to the theft, and acknowledged that the pickup truck that had left the property as I arrived was actually transporting the meat to the Carp freezer plant lockers for storage.

The case was concluded with a conviction and jail sentence within a matter of hours.

Missing Black Angus Steer

Two more cattle rustling cases were reported, one near Stittsville where the farmer was raising black angus cattle. Every few days the farmer would make a count of the number of animals in the field of which he had a record in a book.

The herd was composed of heifers and steers for a total number which seemed to match his book record. On this occasion he decided to just count the steers and to his surprise he was one animal short and immediately reported the loss.

The perimeter fences were checked as well as the neighbours, but no evidence was found that any activity of cattle rustling had taken place. About four days later, the farmer called and stated that he had mistakenly entered the wrong number of steers by one, and when he counted the whole herd, no theft had taken place. Case solved.

Cattle Rustling – Hidden Cow Case

Another cattle rustling case was reported in the North Gower area. A farmer reported that one of his prized milking cows was missing. Again, all the fences around the pasture were checked without any evidence that a theft had taken place.

Again a few days later the farmer reported that he had found the cow in the barn.

The barn door from the pasture entrance was open and the cow had wandered into the barn where they are located in the winter for milking and feeding. Fresh hay had been stored in the front of the feeding area. Somehow the cow decided to check out the hay when the stored hay pile collapsed, burying her under the hay. It took her several days to eat her way out, maybe thirsty, but well fed! Case closed.

Telephone Rip-off in Carp, Ontario

On January 21st, 1951, the Telephone Operator in Carp called to report that the public telephone had been ripped from its mounting in a booth located in front of the rural telephone office.

When I arrived in Carp to investigate, I found that the old style telephone box, which also contained a coin box, had been removed from the booth in front of the office. On checking with the night operator I was advised that a light bulb had recently been replaced and was in good working order. A test showed that the light bulb was in its socket, but was turned out until the bulb lost its contact.

This suggested a person had loosened the bulb to shut the light off before removing the telephone and coin box. Upon dusting for fingerprints, three excellent prints were located burned onto the hot bulb. The bulb was removed and taken to the R.C.M.P. scenes of crime in Ottawa for a possible suspect search.

The Officer in charge of the scenes of crime unit called me within three hours that the search was successful and a suspect had been identified.

The suspect was employed in a Government Office on Sparks Street in Ottawa and as he was ready to leave his employment, I arrested him for the theft. At first he denied being in Carp for more than a month. However, when confronted with the fingerprint evidence that proved he had loosened the bulb just a day or so after the new bulb had been installed, he readily admitted to the theft. At this point I suggested to him, "Let's go to the bridge on 44 highway and I'll fish the telephone and coin box out of the water where you disposed of it." This seemed like the most logical place in the immediate area to get rid of the coin box. To my surprise, that's where I recovered the telephone and coin box. The suspect entered a plea of guilty and was sentenced to a month in jail.

Working in the Ottawa area I was fortunate to have access to the R.C.M.P. scenes of crime lab and could complete my investigation within a six hour period. Although some may consider this to be a minor case, without the help of technology and my trusted camera, fingerprint equipment, and grappling irons this case would not have been solved.

An Unfortunate Rainy Friday Hunting Mishap

A group of men from Ottawa decided to go partridge hunting on a rainy Friday afternoon as they were unable to work at their bricklaying trade due to the rain.

The men decided to go hunting for partridges in the woodlands west of Ottawa. Their plan when they arrived at the location was to form a line about fifty feet apart with their shotguns loaded. This would allow them to cover the area. If a partridge was to take flight, any one of the hunters would be in position to shoot the bird.

Their plan seemed to work when the first partridge took flight. A hunter raised his firearm and took aim following the flight path of the bird. Unfortunately, the partridge made a sharp turn and was parallel with the line of hunters. The hunter who was aiming at the partridge fired at this moment, which had placed his partner in the line of fire. The shot struck the hunter in the head. He died at the scene.

A tragic mishap for the family, as they hadn't been made aware that the bricklayers had gone hunting. As in most cases, the police would go the residence and inform the next of kin. It is usually the investigating officer's duty, as he has the information to answer the questions. It is not a happy moment.

A Spectacular Transport-Tree Collision

A transport truck and trailer unit was traveling north on 16 highway about a mile south of Manotick when the driver allowed his right front wheel of the tractor drive onto the soft shoulder. This swayed the heavy loaded trailer and it overturned sliding off the highway coming to rest on its right side against a large elm tree.

The unusual thing about this collision is how the unit came a stop. As the unit was sliding sideways on its right side the tree became wedged between the tractor and the trailer. The driver did not suffer any injuries and only minor damage occurred to the transport unit.

Another Airplane Crash

Dr. Mount of Ottawa, while flying in a Belanca Monoplane over a field east of the Merivale Road when his airplane motor stalled. Dr. Mount was gliding without power to a landing in the field but overshot the distance and crossed over the Merivale Road under the hydro line heading for a farm house when the wing struck a tree in the front yard of the residence which spun the light plane around as it landed within a few feet of the house, as shown in the photo above. Dr. Mount only suffered a few bruises and walked away from the crash.

A High Impact Collision

Fatal car crash into tree near Acres Road, Highway #15 in 1951

A well known barrister from Ottawa died when the vehicle he was driving crashed head-on into an elm tree within five feet from the edge of the highway near Acres Road on 15 highway. Alcohol and road conditions were not a factor in the collision.

Another Single-Engine Airplane Crash

Another single engine aircraft crashes and burns on impacting the ground. This was a private owner from the Uplands Airport going out on a solo pleasure flight. The cause of the crash was not determined as the pilot perished in the landing and due to the fire destroying the aircraft, no cause could be established.

Assigned to Criminal Investigation Branch

In the fall of 1953 I was transferred to the Ottawa Detachment and assigned to the Criminal Investigation Branch for the next ten years. However, I was still called out to serious vehicle collisions when fatalities occurred. My area of responsibility included all of Carleton County.

This ended my community based service. I was now working with an unmarked car for the most part. During this period I was involved in a number of major criminal investigations, some of which, I will give a brief outline of the events, such as, murders, suicides, armed robberies, crimes against persons, property crimes and serious accidents, such as several more airplane crashes.

Working as an investigator on criminal offences was totally different and more involved. When you investigate a traffic collision the evidence as to how it occurred and who was responsible is right in front of you. In a criminal investigation you have to protect the scene and obtain as much evidence as possible to assist you to locate the responsible person(s).

Working on reports at the Ottawa Detachment Office, 1954

They usually are long gone. This part of my career also brought me in contact with the lives of many people through tragedies and hardships.

The following are stories of some of the investigations that are no longer just a call for service, but require days and even weeks to resolve.

Historical Rape Case

On August 15th, 1954 I was called out in the early morning hours to investigate a rape case involving two 20 year old women and three males ranging in age from 19 to 21 year old.

One of the women had met one of the men earlier, but only knew him by his nick-name. He made a date to pick her up to go to a movie. When he called to pick her up she told him that she had a cousin that had come to visit so, to solve the problem the male person got a friend, and the four went on the date.

When the girls were picked up there was a third male person in the car, and instead of going to the movie they went to a nightclub for a few hours on the Quebec side. They returned to Ottawa and drove out to a pine bush area behind the Ottawa Airport, where the two women were raped by all three of the males.

They really made a mess of the women. The two women came to the detachment to lodge the complaint. They only knew their dates by first names such as Alex, Vic and Len, with a vague description of the car.

One of the males, Vic had printed a telephone number and name "Vic Hobbs" on the arm of one of the women, the name "Hobbs" was not his correct surname it was barely legible but with our special equipment we were able to bring the number up to a legible level.

When I called the number looking for Vic, it happened to be Vic's brother's residence, which was a real stroke of luck. He said his brother lived at another address and also gave a good description of the car, and the correct family surname.

It happened to be Vic's car that was used. With this information Vic was arrested and the car seized from him. I quickly found out who his two male friends were and by evening all three were in custody and charged.

The case made history in the Ottawa Courts as the three suspects were charged jointly; with three defense lawyers and two crown prosecutors we were in for a lengthy trial.

1949 Courthouse

They chose trial by Judge and Jury, so the court empanelled eighty jurors from which twelve were to be chosen. Each of the lawyers and the crown could challenge a juror; unless all four of the lawyers agreed, the juror was released from duty.

This selection took three days with only eleven jurors selected. In Law, the sheriff of the Court can go out on the street and arrest anyone over the age of 21 years and bring them before the court for jury duty.

In this case the sheriff accompanied by two police officers went onto the street and brought six people into the court room, one of these six became the twelfth juror. Imagine going for lunch and being arrested for jury duty and then being involved daily for the next two months at court for three dollars per day and mileage.

The case took six weeks, with a lot of preparation, but in the end all three suspects were given a harsh sentence, collectively twenty years in the penitentiary. It was a widely written up case at the time in the media, Justice Schroeder stated in his remarks before sentencing as follows:

"This case is one of the most sordid and disgusting cases in my experience to try. You have committed the one offence in the Criminal Code, outside of murder, for which the death penalty or life imprisonment may be given." (This was before the death penalty was abolished.)

A Heart Breaking Tragedy

Another case involves a family who were striving to make ends meet. The husband was attempting to make a living with an old dump truck to provide for his wife and four young children.

The wife was seven months pregnant with twins. The truck would break down and was in a garage as many days as it was available to haul gravel so, with no solution in sight and sinking daily deeper into debt, they decided to end it.

On November 6th, 1954 while the four children (aged 2 years to 6 years) were at the grandparents, the final chapter was taking place.

The wife had phoned her mother where the children were at the time telling her the state they were in, that she was trying to talk her husband out of taking his own life, but if she couldn't she would go with him. The grandmother called another relative and when she phoned the house there was no answer so they drove to the farm house and found them in an upstairs bedroom, both shot.

When I arrived with the Coroner Dr. Dowd of Kinburn, the wife was lying on the floor behind the bed with a bullet wound in her forehead, the husband had shot himself in the head as well and rolled off the bed with the .22 cal rifle falling onto his wife, he was still breathing but passed away within a few minutes of our arrival.

The grandmother knew her daughter was pregnant, but was unaware until the autopsy was performed that she was carrying twins. This was a real family tragedy in the community, a case of hard times.

The children were taken care of by the grandmother who was determined to see that they would be well looked after.

Two Suicides In One Day

The next two cases are in a way entwined, even though the victims didn't know each other, they decided to leave this world as if they acted out a pre-determined script in exactly the same way.

On February 2nd, 1956, a farmer in North Gower left his residence to go to another farm nearby where he kept livestock for the winter. It was a daily trip to feed and water the animals.

He apparently had severe headaches and had been concerned about possible cancer. On this date he took a page from the calendar as he walked through the summer kitchen of his home, got into his car and drove to the winter farm.

The barn was fairly large and had a drive through for hay wagons to supply hay to the cattle from inside the barn. He looked after the cattle, wrote a note on the calendar page and left it on the steering wheel of the car.

He then returned to the barn climbed up the to the rafters in the hayloft, tied a rope to a rafter and climbed back down to just above where the wagons would enter. He tied a rope around his neck and swung out over the empty space, committing suicide by hanging. Dr. Dowd of Osgoode the Coroner was called to the scene and the body was removed to the morgue in Ottawa.

When I returned to the Patrol car to sign back on from this investigation the dispatcher said he had another call from a farmer some thirty miles to the west near Kinburn.

When I arrived, the farmer stated that when he was checking on his hired hand he found him in the hayloft area hanging from a rafter. He apparently had committed suicide by hanging. The usual procedure in calling the Coroner to the scene was actioned. Dr. Dowd of Kinburn attended.

The similarities in the previous two cases:

- Two male persons involved.
- Two barns, identical in construction.
- Two hangings by rope from a rafter in the hay storage area.

- Two Coroners attended, both by name of Dr. Dowd (Brothers)
- Second Month of the Year. (February)
- Second day of the Month. (Feb 2nd)
- Both working in the barn looking after livestock.
- Both were depressed.

I call this my famous 222 case, everything was repeated in two's.

The odds of these two cases being duplicated would be astronomically high, if ever.

Another Plane Crash April 2nd, 1956

An RCAF airman was seriously injured when he was forced to crash land his light aircraft in a farmers field near Kinburn. Witnesses reported that the pilot seemed to be in trouble looking for a safe place to land when he crashed into a tree near a deep gully. The impact snapped his seat belt which resulted in injuries to his head, fractured skull and facial damage.

I was given the call to investigate the cause of the crash in conjunction with the RCAF investigators. To get to the crash sight I had to walk across a field and cross a deep gully as the aircraft was on the opposite side from my approach.

I was carrying my camera equipment and had to slowly get to the bottom of the gully which had some snow on the surface and ice under the snow areas, which caused me to slide down to the bottom ending up with a dislocated left shoulder. The Air Force investigators hadn't arrived, so I had to get my shoulder back into its socket, a move I remembered from my first aid training. I was able to put my shoulder back into place and climbed up the side of the gully to the scene of the crash as shown in the photo above.

I finished my work at the scene and drove back to the Ottawa Detachment Office. All in a days work…?

Joy Ride Ends in Tragedy

Two male teenagers had stolen a car and were passing a vehicle at a high rate of speed resulting in a head on collision with an on coming vehicle driven by a 40 year old male person who was instantly killed.

On November 19ᵗʰ, 1956, a stolen car was traveling East on # 17 highway just East of Orleans.

Again an innocent person died because of a joy ride by the teenagers. In this case, they also paid with their lives.

Construction Site Fatality Investigations

Police are called upon to investigate all fatalities, to determine the cause of death. It always bothered me when I had to investigate incidents where the contractor of a project cuts corners by having the workers use equipment and/or material that is unsafe.

The following two examples support my concerns:

A new bridge under construction over the Mississippi river on number 17 highway near Arnprior.

The bridge was being assembled with steel framing with all the joints being riveted. The problem was in the poor quality of the wood used in the scaffolding. The overhead joints had to have a wood scaffold erected to allow the workers to stand on while riveting the framing joints.

The wood used was a poor grade with knots as large as 2 inches in the 2X6 planks; this removed the strength by fifty percent. With two men and the riveting equipment on such a platform of knotted wood planks which was held up by ropes, it was inviting an accident to happen, and it did. When the plank broke at the location of the knot it allowed the platform to slide off the ropes and the men and equipment fell into the river below.

One of the workers struck his head against the steel frame and died at the scene. The foreman attempted to hide the wood used for the platform which I seized. At the Coroner's inquest it only took the Jury ten minutes to reach its verdict that the contractor was responsible.

The Second Fatality Again Caused by Poor Material

Hydro Poles were being erected by a private contractor on a site about 1,500 feet from the main power line.

Seventy foot hydro poles were being erected about 150 feet apart. The usual hole was drilled in the ground for a pole to be anchored, with a cross arm bolted near the top of the pole, a small cable was strung through a pulley, which had been fastened to the cross arm, then the pole was erected which now had the pole standing anchored and the cable hanging from the pulley.

One end of the cable was fastened to a chair lift, while the other end of the line was strung through another pulley fastened at the base of the pole which was then fastened to a jeep type truck about 75 feet from the pole.

You now have a system that allowed you to take equipment to the top of the pole such as the power line fasteners, etc, and a person to sit in the chair with equipment to be transported like an elevator to the top of the pole to accommodate this. The set up would be the same for each pole erected for easy access until the power line wires are installed.

Sounds great except for two major considerations. There is a difference between a straight pull and a jerk pull by the Jeep driver. The pulleys should not be of the cast iron type.

Tests proved that you could pull more than twice the weight by a steady pull as you could by a jerk type pull. This is what happened when the rigger sat into the chair with his gear, about a weight of 350 lbs, and was being pulled up to the top. All it took was the jeep driver hitting the brake pedal hard to stop creating a tension jerk increasing the weight three fold, snapping the cast iron eye of the pulley. This dropped the rigger to the ground with a crushing force, he died instantly.

I built a replica of the system and took it with me to the coroner's jury inquest to demonstrate it to the jury.

The coroner and members of the jury expressed their appreciation.

These two cases are an example of how the rights of the victims and their families must be protected.

The evidence clearly showed that the use of inadequate equipment to save a few dollars contributed to the death of the two breadwinners for the families involved.

I felt that my involvement contributed to the future support of the families and improved inspections of construction sites.

These investigations shows another area of the police involvement in the communities.

Train/Truck collision

A train/truck collision at the railway crossing in Stittsville occurred on March 21st, 1957.

DRIVER DIES IN CRASH—The driver of a highway transport was killed when his heavy truck smashed broadside into a freight car on the CPR crossing in Stittsville early today. Top photo shows the freight car lying on its side across the road after the crash. In the bottom photo, The Dominion, crack CPR passenger train, moves slowly past the wreckage a few hours after the accident. Eastbound from Vancouver to Montreal, it was the first train through after the tracks were cleared.
(Journal photos by Dominion Wide)

This was a normal box car drop off, the freight train would stop with box cars blocking the crossing and uncouple a car to be shunted onto a siding filled with produce for Stittsville to be unloaded. In the meantime a transport truck loaded with produce heading north failed to stop for the flashing lights at the crossing and hit the parked boxcar on the crossing with such an impact that it dumped the boxcar over on its side still coupled see (photo at top). The driver of the transport was killed.

Two More Major Airplane Crashes

The next two cases involve airplane crashes. On May 15th, 1956 a CF-100 was sent out to check on an unidentified aircraft, however something went terribly wrong. The CF-100 crashed into a Grey Nuns Convalescent Home at Orleans, a few miles east of Ottawa in Gloucester Township.

The Convalescent Home was a large three story building able to accommodate up to fifty or more persons. Its layout was a rectangular building about eight hundred feet south of the Ottawa River with a chapel attached at the centre on the south side.

Villa Saint Louis, May 12, 1956 (Photo: Malek)

The CF-100 crashed into the chapel at a south-north angle, going through the chapel and buried itself 28 feet below the basement floor exploding the total building into an inferno. Approximately 25 Grey Nun Sisters were saved, but eleven perished, as well as the cook,

Villa Saint Louis, May 15, 1956, just after crash (Journal photo: Howell)

the two pilots of the aircraft and Father Ward, for a total of fifteen dead.

The building was totally demolished, with the fire so intense that the 11 victims that were trapped inside were completely burned beyond recognition.

Rear view at height of fire (Journal photo: Howell)

Father Ward who was just at the north entrance about to leave for the night, was thrown about fifty feet to the north of the entrance and perished from the impact.

It was a lengthy inquest and investigation, the causal factor of the crash could not be established. My first report was forty-two pages long, and my time spent at the scene was more than six days, anywhere from sixteen to twenty hours per day.

Gus Wersch, Ont. Prov. Police Officer was lead investigator of this disaster...Seen in center photo upper right corner in uniform. May 15, 1956.

Walter Rabbe, a resident near the St Louis rest home, tells Ontario Provincial Police Constable Gus Wersch how he saw the burning jet aircraft explode into the Grey Nuns convent. "It was like a ball of fire rushing out of the sky," said Mr. Rabbe (Photo: Newton)

Bomber Crashes Near Manotick

Almost a year later at about seven in the evening on March 1ˢᵗ 1957, a Mitchell Bomber that had been converted to a service transport aircraft was about to land at the Ottawa Airport. However, the pilot was asked to make another turn in a holding pattern as other flights were landing.

The pilot circled around to the west and was heading back about eight miles south-west of the airport when a part of the fuselage broke off and the plane crashed through a large stand of elm trees. All eight persons on board perished in the crash, debris was scattered for over 1500 feet. The impact was so severe that only small pieces of the craft or the persons were strewn about to be picked up. No determination was made as to the cause.

Converted Mitchell Bomber

GRIM REMINDER OF CRASH—Provincial Constable Gus Wersch (right) examines the battered and burned remnants of an officer's dress hat found amidst the scattered debris at the scene of last night's air tragedy. The man on the left was one of the RCAF investigators. His name was not obtained (Photo: Newton)

During the Years from 1949 to 1964 I investigated 9 air crashes in the area, which seemed rather a high number compared to the number that have taken place since. Most of the air crashes were single engine passenger or training craft related to Uplands Airport in Ottawa.

Halloween Pranksters Get Concrete Punishment

Another Halloween damage to property occurred in one of the west end Townships of Carleton County. Two women from Ottawa had purchased a farm which had a large old log barn still in good condition. The women hired a contractor to removed the stalls to pour a wall to wall concrete floor. The job was completed about eight in the evening on Halloween night. After the contractor left, with no one at the farm about nine teenagers decided to have some of their so called fun by sticking steel scraps, rocks and other items into the freshly poured concrete.

All the items were hardened into the cement when I arrived to investigate about eleven in the morning the following day. I had stopped a car on Halloween night in the area and from the licence plate I obtained the registered owner. To my good fortune the owner of the car had a teenager who proved to be the weakest link in the investigation. Within half an hour I had all the names of the others involved.

To avoid criminal charges and ruin the nine teenagers with a criminal record, I got all the parents together and they agreed to hire the contractor to remove the damaged concrete, the youths had to work with wheel barrows to cart the broken concrete to a gully nearby. All this was done under supervision of two of the parents and with the approval of the victims.

The victims wrote a letter to the Commissioner in Toronto for which I received a letter of appreciation for job well done. It also benefited me while working in the area in subsequent years as the farming community had the greatest respect for the police after that.

Community Bootlegger

Bootlegging was another interesting part of my work. I was the only officer in the area to be issued a blanket warrant. That meant that I carried a special card of authority to search any suspect premises without having to get a warrant from the Justice of the Peace, which saved time if you had to act immediately. Two women were known to be operating bootlegging establishments in Carleton County area. A number of attempts had been made without success of apprehension before I arrived in Ottawa. It was a challenge to see who could apprehend them first. One of the main ingredients to prove a bootlegging case was that you had to prove that there was an unusual amount of traffic to and from the residence.

To establish this at the residence of Marie Flora, I hid in a ditch opposite the residence and across the road from the entrance. The ditch had a good growth of bull rushes which helped to conceal myself and from this vantage point I was able to take note of licence plates of vehicles and even hear conversations. A number of times I could see the owner, Marie Flora, go to a few old cars in the yard and carry packages back to the house. The only discomfort I had occurred while I was lying in the ditch, and felt a small animal crawl over my back. No doubt it was as surprised as I was.

After I had gathered sufficient information, extra officers were called to the scene and the warrant was executed. Enough liquor and beer was located to establish a charge of bootlegging. Marie Flora was convicted and her place was declared a Public Place by the Courts, which meant that she could not have alcoholic beverages on the premises and any police officer could drop in without a warrant to search without notice. This declaration closed her down, as well as having to pay a hefty fine.

Another Bootlegger

The other bootlegger was located about ten miles to the South of Ottawa by the name of "Ma O'Conner".

This was again a private residence which was located in such a way that surveillance was difficult. However, after a few evenings staking out the house we gathered sufficient information to search the premises. After everything was searched, a problem quickly presented itself. We could not find any excess alcohol in the house. While talking to Ma O'Conner in the kitchen, I noticed the refrigerator turning off and on repeatedly making a hollow like sound.

On pulling the refrigerator forward, the back panel was loose with all the insulation missing, which in its place was loaded with liquor, mostly 13 ounce size bottles which were sold to teenagers going to the Saturday night dance in Metcalfe. We had patrol cars apprehend several cars with teenagers that had left the residence and confiscated the liquor as evidence.

Ma O'Connor was charged and convicted and her residence declared a Public Place which put her out of business.

Another Tragic Cigarette Fire

Another tragic investigation involved a fire in Manotick at the Armstrong General Store. The Armstrong family had recently lost their father who passed away as a result of a heart attack, which left the mother and three sons to continue the business. Two were still going to school.

The school bus stopped outside the store to pick up all the high school students that gathered at this focal point. Just before the school bus arrived some of the students were smoking in the store and apparently a cigarette butt was flicked over the counter falling into a box of fire crackers. This set off a burst of explosions with an immediate intense fire…everyone escaped except Mrs. Armstrong as she went up stairs to get some items of value from their second storey residence above the store; she never escaped.

The fire burned quickly and destroyed the building. In the search for any remains, it seemed that any trace of Mrs. Armstrong would not be found. I did find a small item that looked like charred tissue, about 3 inches like a rubber ball. I had this forwarded to the Toronto Forensic Laboratory who concluded that the item was the remains of a human heart which established that Mrs. Armstrong had perished.…a sad ending for the family.

Smoke billows from Manotick store ruins

Working Alone Without Back-up

The police officers of the day worked alone without immediate back-up. This can be tricky, especially when you work an area the size of Carleton County… a few examples come to mind.

Example one – Dance at Constance Bay, Torbolton Township, a Hall called the Casino where usually a large crowd of the area's younger set attended, and without fail, liquor and beer were brought in to liven up the activity, which ended up with disturbances. Police were called and guess who responded? A single officer in the midst of at least 250 persons with no back-up. You isolated the trouble makers and got them to leave the area. The thing that protected you was the uniform. You were still respected in those days and the uniform represented respect.

Example two – How do you protect yourself when you are alone in the middle of the night patrolling the area and you receive a call from the dispatcher to check out a maintenance shed on the railway a thousand feet or so from the highway at Manotick Station. The message goes on to state two dangerous criminals escaped from Kingston penitentiary and a report was received that two persons were walking along the rail line in the Manotick Station area. My order was to check out the maintenance shed in case they are seeking refuge in this shed for the night.

Problem… no back-up and you have to walk a thousand feet along the railway line to get to the shed's location. How do you prepare yourself? What I did at the time was to prepare myself for self defence. It was in winter and we wore the old style "Pea Jacket" which had a large pocket on the right side. The only weapon I had was a loaded revolver with six bullets.

I removed the revolver from my holster from under my Pea Jacket and removed my glove from my right hand, took the revolver and placed it into the Pea Jacket pocket and held it with my right hand on the ready, to shoot if necessary, through the pocket while I approached the shed. As it turned out the shed was empty and I returned to my patrol car to continue my night patrol. Because you worked alone you had to prepare for any emergency and not become a statistic in the newspaper.

I was involved in a number of confrontations during my tours of duty without back-up while on patrol; you just handled the situations as best you could to prevent the confrontation from escalating by using the most useful weapon "Common Sense Persuasion".

Other Investigations of Interest

A stolen vehicle investigation in the area led to finding the station wagon overturned in a field approximately 200 feet from the road near Kars, Ontario. It required a tow truck to right the vehicle and remove it. On checking the area where the vehicle was removed from, a wallet was found with identification documents of the person (who, no doubt, stole the vehicle) living in Manotick. When I arrived at the residence I was met by a freshly bruised individual, and when shown his wallet he admitted to the theft and was subsequently convicted of car theft.

Carp Post Office Break-In and Safe Cracking in 1954

Located in the village of Carp, Ontario, the thieves entered by breaking open a hole into the rear of the block stone wall. Due to it being a weekend, no one in the immediate area heard or saw any activity. The area where the post office safe was located was in a mess with broken concrete from the wall and around the safe. Money and postage stamps were stolen.

On investigation at the scene three wrecking bars were left behind, and by sifting through the rubble, some small pieces of heavy wrapping paper were found with a name of a hardware store printed on it

The hardware store was identified in Hull, Quebec with its name as advertisement embedded on the paper wrapping. A senior store clerk identified the paper as coming from their store. He had made note of the licence plate of the vehicle that a well dressed man left in after purchasing three wrecking bars of similar size that were sold to him on the Saturday before the Carp Post office break in.

The owner of the vehicle was a well known criminal living in Montreal. He was arrested and charged.

North Gower Royal Bank Branch Armed Robbery on December 8, 1954

Three armed men tied up the bank manager and staff, removed approximately $33,000 in cash and a revolver, then fled in a stolen car which was recovered in Ottawa. Subsequent investigation led to the arrest of one individual in Montreal as well as a second person now known to the police was sought. The revolver and most of the stolen money was not recovered. Some thirty years later a firearm was recovered in Montreal and its origin was investigated. Information was circulated that this revolver was taken from an armed robbery in eastern Ontario.

I received a call from the Ontario Provincial Police in Toronto at the Nepean Police Station where I was now located as Chief of Police for the city of Nepean. I always saved my notebooks, and on checking the 1954 book, I found the incident with the serial number of the revolver. This information ended with the official closure of the case.

Accidental Fatal Shooting at Constance Bay in January 1957

I received a call at the Ottawa Detachment that a fatal gun shot accident had occurred. A contractor from the Kinburn, Ontario area, along with some of his construction workers went to relax at his cottage in Constance Bay. The contractor decided to check on some animal tracks in the snow nearby, taking along two long guns, a .303 Rifle and a 410 shotgun. He was alone at the time as his friends remained in the cottage.

His footprints in the snow indicated that he had walked about 400 feet to a small clearing which was a pond covered with ice and about 10 inches of new snow. He apparently stopped, as something caught his attention; he decided to stand the shot gun into the snow butt down (a hunter never places the barrel down so it can't get blocked).

The marks indicated that the snow was too soft to support the shotgun and after several butt marks in the snow, the shotgun discharged and struck him in his throat under the jaw. Marks in the snow indicated he was temporarily knocked out and on recovering he crawled about 200 feet back towards the cottage and died.

The conclusion of this incident played out in another direction; it involved the personal insurance payment to the family as the insurance company decided it was a suicide and that the coverage did not apply.

My report from the hands on investigation supported that this was an accident.

The insurance company sent two representatives to my office to convince me that this was a suicide and that they did not intend to pay the policy seeking my support for their theory. From the investigation, I concluded that the shotgun had been cocked and loaded; when the contractor, in a downward thrust to make the firearm stand in the snow, the impact jarred the mechanism to discharge, with the gun barrel aligning its angle upward to have the shot strike him in the throat.

I knew that there would be a disagreement, so I decided to set the stage to repeat the contractors action in my office as a demonstration. I pre-tested the 410 by removing the contents of two 410 shotgun shells from the scene, cutting the paper casing off only leaving the cap portion and about half an inch of the shell casing. When I inserted this empty casing into the gun, cocked it, and struck the floor with the butt, it discharged. My conclusion was that the firearm mechanism was worn and allowed the cocked gun to discharge on impacting the butt on a hard surface which resulted in this tragedy.

I then prepared the second shell by removing its contents as in the above test, loaded the firearm and had it available to show the insurance investigators.

At the meeting the insurance investigators wouldn't accept my theory of the discharge mishap, so I told them that I would demonstrate it to them. I took the 410 shot gun, cocked it and struck the butt of the shotgun onto the floor. This caused the gun to discharge with the loud explosion. Not knowing that I had a live cartridge in the gun, they almost fell of their chairs.

Needless to say, the insurance was paid to the family.

ONTARIO PROVINCIAL POLICE

The above Cap Badge and Collar Dogs were issued
to Ewart Gus WERSCH on graduation from the
Ontario Police College on December 19th, 1949 at
Ajax Ontario.

Along with these insignia's a warrant card No. 1698
was issued identifying my being sworn in as an
Officer of the Ontario Provincial Police, to have the Authority
to Serve in the Province of Ontario, as a Peace Officer.

The Cap Badge and Collar Dogs were worn by me from
December 19th, 1949 until my voluntary resignation from
the Provincial Police on January 12th, 1964 to join the
Nepean Township Police Force.

Commissioner Eric Silk of the Ontario Provincial Police
Authorized that Cap Badge and Collar Dogs were to be
retired with me as a memento of my Service.

Ewart Gus Wersch

ONTARIO

THE ATTORNEY GENERAL

Toronto, Ontario,
March 11th, 1963.

Constable E. G. Wersch,
Ontario Provincial Police Detachment,
OTTAWA, Ontario.

Dear Constable Wersch,

You will recall that, on the last day of the Advance Investigation Course at the Ontario Provincial Police School here on Sherbourne Street, I had the pleasure of speaking to the class and then meeting each of you as we had our pictures taken.

I enjoyed this occasion very much and was very pleased indeed to have had the opportunity of meeting each of those chosen by their District Inspector to attend this Course.

I thought that you might like to have the enclosed photograph as a momento of our meeting on that day.

I would like to add my best wishes also for your continued success as a member of the Ontario Provincial Police which is an organization of which we can certainly be very proud.

Yours sincerely,

Attorney General.

FMC:ms
Encl.

ONTARIO

ONTARIO PROVINCIAL POLICE FORCE
OFFICE OF THE COMMISSIONER

FOREWORD

This volume contains Standing Orders issued for the government and general guidance of the Ontario Provincial Police Force.

Standing Orders are general orders of a more or less permanent nature. They may, as circumstances require, be augmented or enlarged by circular memoranda or directive from time to time.

No set of rules can be drawn up that will meet every situation and no matter how detailed Orders may be, something must be left to the intelligence and discretion of the officer concerned. Members of the Ontario Provincial Police are therefore expected to interpret these instructions reasonably and with due regard to the interests of the Force.

The primary duties of every law enforcement officer consists of the protection of life and property, the prevention of crime, the apprehension of offenders and the preservation and maintenance of the public peace. Crime has no business hours and it is only by maintaining a constant state of preparedness and vigilance that a police organization can successfully combat it. To achieve this end it is imperative that all members of the Ontario Provincial Police Force carry out their duties energetically and faithfully at all times.

R. V. McNeill

Commissioner of Police for Ontario.

Toronto, Ontario,
April 1st, 1954.

Introduction page from a 118 page Standing Orders issued by the Ontario Provincial Police April 1st 1954 (a copy of the Standing Orders issued to Provincial Cst. Gus Wersch has been retained as an historical item). There are many more stories in my service in the provincial police. However my police career continued in the Nepean Township Police Area in Carleton County, which was part of my original beginning in 1949.

A New Beginning

I left the Provincial Police and joined the Nepean Police Force on January 13th, 1964 which will be continued in a separate segment to my service which eventually ended with my retirement on May 31st, 1988, a few months short of 39 years Police Service

Photographs below show the different Police Forces.

Prov.Constable Ewart Gus Wersch
Nov. 1st,1949–Jan.12th,1964
Age 22 years

Sgt. Ewart Gus Wersch
Jan.13th, 1964–Apr.1st 1966
Nepean Township Police

Chief of Police Ewart Gus Wersch
Nepean Twp. Police
Apr 1,1966–Nov 1978
City of Nepean Police
Nov. 1978–May 31st 1988

The Police Service in Nepean moving forward

Behind the Badge

PART THREE

~ CHAPTER 7 ~

Nepean Police Force
1964–1994

Introduction of Police Services Leading up to 1964

On January 13th, 1964, after having served with the Ontario Provincial Police from November 1st, 1949 to January 12th, 1964, I started my employment with the Nepean Township Police Force.

Nepean Township was the major municipality in Carleton County and the fastest growing in industry and population. A short history of the Township of Nepean is as follows:

Prior to 1945 Nepean had a population base of approx. 21,000 residents which was mainly from the expansion of the north east section adjoining Ottawa. The Provincial Police were mainly a rural and major highway patrol Force and did not police areas with over 5,000 population, so it became necessary for Nepean to form a separate Police Force for the north east corner of Nepean.

The first Nepean Police Force was established for the area known as Westboro in 1945, with Borden Conley being appointed as the first Nepean Township Chief of Police, with a staff of approximately eight officers. The remainder of Nepean continued to be served by the Provincial Police as the population had been reduced to approximately 2,700 residents.

On January 1st, 1950, Ottawa annexed the Westboro area of Nepean, including the Police Force, which became part of the Ottawa Police Force.

It was on December 19th, 1949 that I came to the Ottawa Detachment area, as a member of the Ontario Provincial Police. Nepean and the adjoining Township of Gloucester to the east were again growing at a rapid pace, well over the 5,000 population level, so again these two municipalities had to form their own Police Force.

The governing bodies of the two Townships decided to form a joint Police Force known as the Gloucester-Nepean Township Police Force.

The Provincial Police continued to serve the remaining eight townships and villages within Carleton County, as well as the Provincial Highways running through Gloucester and Nepean into Ottawa.

The Gloucester-Nepean Township Police was established on July 1st, 1957 under the command of Chief John Rankin. This union was a difficult one, in that the Rideau River divided the two Municipalities, no bridges, and Nepean was growing at about three to one in businesses and population.

The sharing of the financial costs became a nightmare, which resulted in a continuous argument at meetings, to such an extent that the two Municipalities decided to go it alone. The joint force was dissolved with each Municipality establishing their own Police Force on January 1st, 1964.

This was a new beginning for the Nepean Police Service that lasted for the next thirty years until Jan 1st, 1994.

By-Law No. 73-63 was enacted by the Nepean Township Council of the day to establish a Police Service in and for the Township of Nepean to be effective on January 1st,1964

CORPORATION OF THE TOWNSHIP OF NEPEAN

By-Law No. 73-63

A By-Law to establish a Police Force in
the Township of Nepean, in the County of
Carleton.

- - - - -

WHEREAS the Police Act, R.S.O. 1960, Chapter
298, as amended, authorized Council to establish a Police
Force,

NOW THEREFORE the Council of the Corporation
of the Township of Nepean in the County of Carleton,
hereby enacts as follows:

1. There shall be in the Township of Nepean
   a Police Force consisting of one or more
   constables or other police officers
   appointed by Council.

2. The Council may appoint a Chief Constable.

3. The Council will provide for the management
   and operation of the Police Force.

4. The Police Force to be established and
   effective on the 1st day of January, 1964,
   is to be known as the Nepean Township Police
   Department.

PASSED AND GIVEN under the Hands of the Reeve
and Clerk and the Corporate Seal of the Municipal Corporation
of the Township of Nepean this 28th day of November, 1963.

_____
Clerk

_____
Reeve

ONTARIO

EXECUTIVE COUNCIL OFFICE

OC-3778/65

Copy of an Order-in-Council approved by His Honour the Lieutenant Governor, dated the 21st day of October, A.D. 1965.

Upon the recommendation of the Honourable the Attorney General, the Committee of Council advise that pursuant to the provisions of sub-section 1, of Section 7 of the Police Act, R.S.O. 1960, Chapter 298, as amended by Section 2 of the Police Amendment Act, 1965, Chapter 99, a Board of Commissioners of Police be established for the Township of Nepean, and that His Honour Judge A.E. Honeywell, Judge of the County Court in and for the County of Carleton, and Magistrate H.G. Williams, Q.C. of Ottawa, Ontario, be designated as Members of the aforementioned Board, effective the 1st day of November, 1965.

Certified -- Clerk, Executive Council.

First Police Commission

Reeve A. Moodie -- Chairman
His Honour Judge A.E. Honeywell -- Member
Magistrate H.G. Williams, Q.C. -- Member

THE ABOVE IS A COPY OF THE ORIGINAL

NEPEAN POLICE FORCE:
A New Beginning Jan 1st, 1964.

We now arrive at that moment in time when Nepean will have its own established Police Force which will be around for the next thirty years. The officers of the joint Force, Gloucester and Nepean, were released and had the option to apply to either Municipality, Chief John Rankin and seventeen officers came to Nepean.

Two police officers from the Ottawa Detachment of the Ontario Provincial Police along with one civilian and a part time clerk stenographer were added to the New Township Police Force.

Photo of Nepean Police Staff as of January 1964
Top Row: *Cpl. Ron Elstone, Cpl. Bud Henry, Sgt. E. Gus Wersch, Chief John Rankin. Cpl. Walter Chaykowski, Cpl. Robert Behan, and Cst. William Dalton*
Center Row: *Cst. Richard Chapman, Cst. Peter Monette, Cst. James Sheahan, Ms. Shirley Gordon, Cst. Fred Gardner, Cst. William Taylor, Cst. Keith Morrill*
Bottom Row: *Cst. Willard Storey, Cst. Robert Mancuso, Cst. Nyall Parks, Cst. Arthur Lewis, Cst. Ron Driscoll, Cst. John Ethier, Mr. William Kerr, Cst. Wayne Phillips*

Chief John Rankin
Nepean Township Police 1964–1966.

Sergeant Gus Wersch
Nepean Township Police 1964.

I had established my roots in Nepean while serving the Carleton County area, which included Nepean. As a member of the Ontario Provincial Police and because Nepean was accepting additional applicants, I applied, and was immediately accepted and appointed to the position as second in charge, holding the rank of Sergeant in the newly established police force.

One additional officer and a part time stenographer were hired, which established the strength of the Force at twenty officers and two civilians. We were ready to meet the day to day challenges in a Municipality of 35,266 residents adjoining the City of Ottawa, Ontario.

NEPEAN SWEARING IN CEREMONY—Five policemen of the newly-formed Nepean township Police Department surround their Chief, John Rankin, following the swearing in ceremony by County Magistrate Austin O'Connor at the Court House Tuesday. Pictured from left to right are Cpl. Walter Chaykowski, Constable Keith Morrill, Det. William Dalton, and Constables Fred Gardiner and Ronald Driscoll. Seated is Chief Rankin.

Nepean Township Police Station
Basement Floor, 1683 Merivale Road

Nepean Police Accommodation January 1964 to November 1966
Located at 1683 Merivale Road – front view or the main floor of the Health Unit.

Photo at left shows entrance to basement floor where the Nepean Police shared part of the basement with the Health Unit.

The first order of the day was to move into our new police accommodations. We were assigned the lower floor of the health unit consisting of three offices and a storage room at 1683 Merivale Road in the centre of the built up area. As most of the officers had policing experience in Nepean, it was relatively easy to adapt to the territory. This was a temporary location.

The accommodation supplied by the Township of Nepean in the basement of the County Health Unit at 1683 Merivale Road wasn't adequate.

As can be seen from the above photo, it was like being in a dungeon and didn't provide for privacy in dealing with the public. Within a year, plans had been drafted for a new Nepean Township Hall to be built at 3825 Richmond Road, Bells Corners.

The new township hall had provisions for the accommodation of the Nepean Township Police, which was officially opened in the fall of 1966. The Nepean Township Police moved to their new quarters and remained at this location until November 28th, 1978.

I was appointed in charge of Operations and with my fourteen plus years of experience in all phases of police work, it was amazing how quickly all the duties and assignments were up and running. For the most part, the residents were hardly aware of the change, except in the name and more visibility of the police service in the area.

The first three months of involvement were setting up the patrol zones and scheduling officers to these areas. We set up four platoons with one of the Corporals in charge with a complement of three Patrol Officers. The Corporal would be assigned to one of the patrol zones, but also had the extended duty to visit the total area as the Supervisor and assist the Patrol Officers in any zone should the investigation require assistance.

The general complaints and traffic collision investigations were handled along with investigating criminal incidents of a minor nature.

Two officers were assigned to the more serious extended criminal investigations as well as assisting the Patrol Officers.

The officer in charge of the Field Operations was the Sergeant who also reviewed the reports submitted by the Field Officers to make sure that all possible action had been taken to resolve the incident or complaint.

The civilian Mr. William Kerr, was assigned to the information desk and dispatched calls for service to the Patrol Units.

The Chief Of Police was in charge of the Administration of the Police Service, and reported the activity to the Nepean Police Commission at a monthly meeting. He reviewed the need for additional staff or other support if the work load exceeded the police ability to serve the community properly, plus all other office duties as preparing the annual budget and dealing with the business community.

After two short years the Nepean Township suffered its first loss of an officer.

On January 30th, 1966 Chief John Rankin had passed out at his residence as he was about to leave for work and was rushed to the Civic Hospital. He was diagnosed as having a malignant brain tumor and had to have an operation. He never came out of a coma and passed away on March 12th, 1966.

Chief John Rankin, a native of Scotland, was a Detective Sergeant in the Glasgow City Police before he came to Canada in 1947.

His first two police involvements in Canada were as Chief of Police for Madoc, Ontario, followed by joining the police in Morrisburg, again as Chief of Police. These were two or three man Police Forces. Later, he was hired by the newly formed Gloucester-Nepean Township Police effective, July 1st, 1957.

When the joint Gloucester-Nepean Township Police divided to form their own Township Police Departments, Chief John Rankin chose to join the Nepean Township Police with 17 officers of the joint Police Department in 1964.

During Chief Rankin's brief illness, Sgt. Ewart Gus Wersch was appointed Acting Chief of Police for Nepean as of February 8th, 1966, on an interim basis until Chief Rankin was able to return. However this was not to be, Chief John Rankin passed away.

Sgt. Ewart Gus Wersch who was an experienced police officer having served in Carleton County since 1949 as his first posting to the Ottawa Detachment of the Provincial Police, and when the Gloucester-Nepean Township Police separated he joined the Nepean Police Department in charge of operations, bringing with him 15 years of experience in field operations with the last ten years as a Criminal Investigator for the OPP in Carleton County.

Acting Chief Ewart Gus Wersch was appointed Chief of Police for the Township of Nepean on April 1st 1966 by the Nepean Police Commission.

Ewart Gus Wersch appointed to Chief of Police for Nepean Township April 1st, 1966–1988

I served as the Chief of Police for the Township of Nepean from April 1st 1966 to November 28th, 1978 and when the Nepean Township changed its status to the City of Nepean. I continued to serve as the Chief of Police for the City of Nepean until May 31st, 1988, for a total of 22 plus years in this position, until my retirement.

The officers that joined the Nepean Police from the joint force had little or no training, so it became a great need to establish a training program. We could only afford to send one or two officers to the Ontario Police College at a time, but in a matter of two years, we were able to upgrade all the officers. It took some overtime by others to free officers to attend, but it was worth the effort.

The following report will highlight some of the major traffic collisions and criminal activity.

CN Railway Hand Car and Vehicle Collision

The first major traffic collision took place on March 13th, 1964, at the CNR crossing on Woodroffe Avenue, a mile or so south of the Baseline Road. Employees of the CNR were traveling west on a " handcar" and as they were crossing the roadway a vehicle collided with the "handcar" toppling the handcar into the ditch and demolishing the motor vehicle.

Three employees of the CNR on the hand car were killed. The driver of the motor vehicle received extensive injuries but survived. One of the other two CNR employees on the handcar died in the hospital and two others survived.

Investigation showed that the handcar would not be able to trip the signal lights, but regulations were in force that the operator of a hand car when arriving at a crossing must stop and have one person act as a flagman, as well as making sure that it was safe to cross. This wasn't done and resulted in four persons losing their lives.

The CNR line is a major route heading west from Ottawa through the heart of Nepean Township crossing a number north-south roadways – Merivale Road, Woodroffe Avenue, Cedarview Road, number 15 Provincial Highway, Moodie Drive – every mile or so. It is expected that many more lives will be lost before overpasses are built.

A Coroner's jury enquiring into the fatal collision concluded that the CNR employees failed to follow regulations and that the motor vehicle driver was travelling at a greater speed than required at the crossing. The Jury concluded that both parties were equally at fault.

Cst. Ronald Driscoll who was the principal investigator assisted by other officers at the scene testified at the Inquest.

The following photograph and description is an accurate account of the circumstances leading to this tragic loss of life. (Photograph and accompanying description was obtained from the local newspaper of the day.)

The names of individuals involved were public knowledge, as they were published in the newspaper of the day.

Three Killed, Two Injured In Nepean Crash

Three CNR employees were killed and two other persons were injured in a collision of a railway handcar and an automobile on Woodroffe Avenue, a mile south of Base Line Road shortly after 9 a.m. today.

The dead, all passengers on the westbound handcar, were identified as:

Willis White, of Goulbourn Township;

Tony Perrier, of Moose Creek, and,

John Passaw, of Renfrew.

Injured are:

James Kenneth McLean, Box 441, Bell's Corners in critical condition with head injuries and compound fractures of both legs and,

Malcolm Massey, 34, of Manotick, in good condition with facial injuries.

"It was a terrible sight," said Malcolm Kosmack, who watched, horror-stricken as the handcar was hurtled from the track and flipped into the ditch.

"Two of the men were thrown right out and the other two landed underneath it," he said.

Driver of the northbound car was helped from the car by Mr. Kosmack and other persons who arrived within minutes of the collision.

Constable Ron Driscoll was the lead investigator

The second fatal collision took place on May 4th, 1964 at 6:55 am

Truck Wrecked

Richmond Man Killed in Crash At Rail Crossing

By ERIC BENDER
of The Journal

A level crossing accident at Cedar View Road and the CNR tracks at Bell's Corners claimed the life of a milk delivery man at 7 a.m. today.

Dead is Wayne Aptt, 22, of Richmond, delivery man in Lynwood Village for Producer's Dairy. He is the father of a five-month-old baby.

TRUCK DEMOLISHED

"You couldn't have a car or truck smashed up any worse," said veteran police sergeant Gus Wersch of Nepean Police. "In other words, if it was any worse you wouldn't find anything."

Mr. Aptt's body was found more than 400 feet west of the crossing. His truck was smashed almost beyond recognition.

Police said the train had been travelling at between 50 and 55 miles an hour.

Mrs. James McLean, 58, of 3011 Base Line Road, who lives beside the crossing, said the train was a regular CNR freight express.

A milk truck delivery van drove across the railway crossing at Cedarview Road at approximately 6:55 am and was struck by the engine of the freight train traveling west, totally demolishing the truck, killing the driver.

As we looked into the future it was evident that many more lives would be lost as this CNR railway crosses many motor vehicle roads leading into the City of Ottawa, which will only escalate as the traffic increases.

The Coroner's Jury concluded that automatic signals should be installed at the Cedarview Road CNR crossing. They also concluded that the CNR maintenance building near the crossing was a vision factor. Constable Wayne Phillips was the lead investigator in this instance. The freight train had to be uncoupled to allow motor vehicle traffic to cross as this had become a major local access road to Ottawa nearby. The remainder of 1964 saw an increase in the calls for service, such as a drowning of a nine year old girl in a quarry, motor vehicle collisions, break-ins and thefts, as the population increased. The Nepean Police complement was working many overtime hours and required additional staff to cope with the urban patrol areas and investigations.

The Nepean Police involvement in the community in 1965 showed an increase of commercial break-ins. As businesses expanded into the urban area, it became a target for criminals from Ottawa and even Toronto and Montreal to expand their interests to growing communities. They would enter the urban area commit their break-ins and disappear into the larger centres to fence the stolen goods.

Crime prevention programs were initiated with the new commercial ventures, to help them establish security procedures, since we were no longer in an area that could take a "care less" attitude.

****

On January 8th, 1965, our civilian dispatcher Mr. William Kerr passed away from natural causes, he was 65 years old at the time.

Nepean Township's first Board of Police Commissioners November 1st, 1965

On November the 1st, 1965, the Province of Ontario authorized the first Nepean Police Commission, rather than a Committee of council. This removed political involvement in the Governing of the Police Service with the exception of one member of council, in this case it was the Reeve of the Township of Nepean.

His Honor Judge A.E. Honeywell, Reeve D.A. Moodie, Magistrate Harry Williams

Chief John Rankin was laid to rest in the Capital Memorial Gardens in Nepean, Ontario.

Police Officers from Eastern Ontario Police Departments attended the funeral services.

Funeral Parade and cortage for Chief John Rankin March 15th, 1966

New Nepean Township Hall nearing completion

As the new Township of Nepean Town Hall in Bells Corners, was well underway in its construction, the officers looked forward to the move to the new facilities.

The move to larger and more defined accommodation allowed the Nepean Police to set up areas for the Operational Branches.

The building included a cell block for the temporary holding of suspects. This allowed the police to have the opportunity to do the processing in house.

The floor plan of the Nepean police accommodation required some changes to be made in the room layouts as the building progressed.

It was expected to be opened in November of 1966.

Nepean Township Hall opened November 21,1966

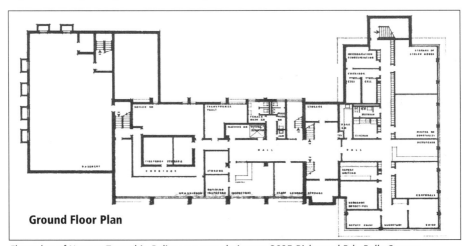

Floor plan of Nepean Township Police accommodations at 3825 Richmond Rd., Bells Corners

We had more room, but the space allotted would become too crowded, which meant that the Nepean Police had to be assigned the total ground floor of the Township Hall within three years.

By the mid 1970's it became an emergent problem for the Council of the day to not only provide the police with more accommodation, but they also had to provide more space for the staff at the Township Hall as the Township was continuing with its rapid growth in population, housing and commercial ventures.

Photograph of bell and stand in front of new Town Hall

Night photo of City Hall in Nepean Township in Bells Corners, 3825 Richmond Road, 1969

Map of the Township of Nepean. Population 45,934 in 1966
Note the top right corner of the map is the area that Ottawa annexed from Nepean in 1950.

Train-Vehicle Collisions Continue

On February 7th, 1966 another train-motor vehicle crash occurred, as expected. It occurred at the crossing at Greenbank Road, again on the same CNR line – a car struck the engine of the train and was bounced off into the ditch demolishing the vehicle, however no fatality resulted.

CNR Train Strikes Youth Playing on Rail Line

Another CNR train, on the same line, a few months later resulted in the death of a four year old boy when he and some playmates entered onto the rail line property. This was a tragic death that perhaps could have been prevented with better fencing and supervision of the children.

The change in the Police accommodation in September 1966, allowed for the following:

In the fall of 1966 a new Nepean City Hall was completed and the Nepean Police Force was housed on the ground floor, still partly below ground. We were slowly coming out of the basement, the windows were a few feet above ground, not a morale booster, but it was new accommodation, with sufficient space for the police, and it was part of the City Hall whereby we could communicate to the other departments in the same building.

The next five to eight years gave us the opportunity to establish a variety of responsibilities within the force structure, to specialize in our training in these various branches and to better serve the needs of the public.

Divisions and Special Branches were established to deal with the variety of responsibilities. Three divisions were established; Administration, Criminal, and Traffic. Each had special units within, such as the Criminal Investigation Branch, Youth, Identification, Training, Traffic, School Patrol and general operation units, underwater search and rescue, a field identification vehicle for crime scenes, snowmobile, dirt bikes, etc.

The officers assigned to these special branches received special training which made the Nepean Police Force fully capable of dealing with all the complaints, from simple by-law infractions to a major crime such as murder.

With 25% of the population being of school age in the Nepean Township area, it necessarily followed that serious attention was required for the protection and safety of the students going to schools which were increasing rapidly to keep up with the population explosion.

A school safety program was organized and a full time School Safety Officer was assigned to work with the school management. School crossing guards were organized at intersections in the school areas to protect the younger students at the numerous crossings.

School Safety Branch Established

Constable John Wilkinson worked many hours to establish the School Safety Patrol system which proved to be invaluable in preventing young children from being injured on our streets, and by following up with lectures in school as well as supervising high usage areas.

From left to right – E.G. Wersch, Chief of Police Nepean Township; Mr. Louis Krygsman, chairman Nepean High School Board; Mrs. Joyce Harris, Chairman Nepean Public School Board; Mr. Vernon Zinck, Chairman of Combined Separate School Board; Cst. John Wilkinson, Nepean Township Police Safety Officer. Cooperation and support in Safety Programme has been given by your School Boards. This coupled together with the parents' participation in further educating the children at home to respect and obey patrol members, and teaching safety rules should go along way in making this a successful programme.

The old Nepean Township Hall was located on Richmond Road west of Churchill Avenue. It had been built in 1896 with a bell tower which housed the infamous bell that was used to call out the fire department or ring on occasion when curfew was declared.

The bell became a focal point in the community.

It was removed reappearing at the new Nepean Township hall in 1966 at Bells Corners.

The story behind the bell removal was a mystery as it was alleged to be taken without official authorization. However, photographs on the following page display the so called removal in progress as follows:

The photographs show the Town Hall, as a fire truck boom is used to access the bell tower, the next photo shows the bell being lowered by a cable, followed by depositing the bell into the back of a pick-up truck

The bell was apparently stored until the new Nepean Township Hall, at 3825 Richmond Road Bells Corners, was completed when it reappeared to be installed in a special stand in front of the new Township of Nepean Town Hall in the fall of 1966.

The bell and stand later became a corporate "Logo" for use by the Township of Nepean in their identification markings on vehicles, stationery, and even on the doors of the police patrol cars and the uniform shoulder flashes of all branches.

Photos of the Westboro-Nepean Township Hall, bell removal and new Township Hall with the bell installed in the fall of 1966 at 3825 Richmond Rd., Bells Corners are shown in the following pages.

When the new Nepean Township Hall was completed in the Fall of 1966, an official opening Ceremony was held in the Council chambers. A rope was tied to the bell, then strung through from the outside to the Council chamber to where the person in charge of the ceremony pulled on the rope which rang the bell as the declaration was made.

A controversy developed in reference to the "Bell" that was used for years in the Nepean Township Hall tower located at 345 Richmond Road, Westboro when it went missing from the tower.

Bell removal in progress

Who took the ding-dong?

Who took the bell?

Bell reappears at new Town Hall
3825 Richmond Road,
Bells Corners

Bell removal from tower

Lowering by boom

Placing in pickup truck to escape the scene?

A two line verse asked the Question:

"Who took the Ding-Dong? Who took the Bell?"

Photographs show how the "Bell" was removed from the tower and for a few months disappeared, then re-appears in the special structure in front of the new Township Hall at Bells Corners. It was used to ring in the new era of Nepean at the Official opening.

The structure was a triangle with three different heights each part of the stand denoting Father, Mother and Child inferring a family community, with the bell hanging from the centre of the triangular structure. The "Bell" was a historical reference to the Township of Nepean history.

The controversial "BELL" removal in progress or a retrieval and the travel from 345 Richmond Road has been solved...

NEPEAN TOWNSHIP HALL and POLICE CENTER
3825 Richmond Rd. Bells Corners.........1966

The "BELL" re-appears, bright and shiny.

Photograph of early Nepean Police patrol cars

The 1960's ......Nepean Township Police Patrol Cars

Sergeant W. Chaykowski discussing events of the day with Chief Gus Wersch in the Chief's office in the new Police accommodation at the Town Hall.

Another program of interest was initiated with the sponsorship of the Nepean City View Kiwanis, which set up a large billboard at a strategic high usage traffic area to inform the residents of monthly traffic statistics. This hopefully helped them not to become a statistic by driving with care and consideration for others using the streets.

The billboard was installed on Merivale Road near Clyde Avenue in a heavy traffic area. Feedback from residents indicated that it was well received and it was used by Community Associations to be mindful of safe driving practices.

Cst. John Wilkinson of the Nepean Police updated the traffic data on a monthly basis. It was a popular and timely way of conveying the message to the residents of Nepean.

Cst. John Wilkinson, Nepean Township Police Safety Officer, posting accident statistics while Chief Wersch looks on.

Billboard established early in 1967 on the Merivale Road near Clyde Avenue, Nepean.

Another Freight Train-Motor Vehicle Collision

Another freight train motor vehicle collision at the Woodroffe CNR crossing. A fuel oil truck slid onto the railroad and was struck by the freight train engine. The truck exploded causing the fuel to be ignited and shot 75 feet into the air. The signal lights were working at the time. The driver was thrown clear of the fire and was rescued from the cab of the truck. He was injured without fatal consequences.

Bicycle Licensing Approved

May 1967 the police requested the Council of the day to authorize a bicycle licensing program which was necessary to cope with identification of recovered stolen or abandoned bicycles. A one dollar fee was charged. The program was well accepted but the licenses were only available from the police station. This created a low response because of the availability to the cyclists.

Efforts were made to fund the project and to waive the one dollar fee by having parents and children register their bicycles at the schools. Information cards were filed for identification and a special sticker was issued to be placed on the bicycle. This turned out to be the answer, as we were able to register hundreds of bicycles. A great percentage of bicycles were returned to the owners within days of being lost or stolen because of this program.

Taxicab Licensing Approved

Effective July 1st 1967 the Nepean Council passed a by-law to have all taxis in Nepean Township licensed.

This became necessary to place some order of control relating to the number of taxis, the maintenance of vehicles to be fit, insured and safe to carry passengers. The drivers were licensed and were required to display their identification to passengers. It also put a control on the drivers to have a qualified chauffeur's license as a safety issue for the passengers. (By-Law 28-67)

Staffing Problems

As we reached the 50,000 mark in the population growth, we were in dire straits to meet the calls for service due to inadequate number of staff. It seemed that the concern was aimed at the cost to provide the service rather than to provide an available and qualified service.

Submissions both before and at budget time were made to increase the staff by a minimum of 12 officers as our ability to provide proper service in the community had deteriorated. Our staff to population ratio of one officer to 1,562 residents was totally inadequate.

Overtime escalated which created extra pressure and fatigue on the officers and their families' welfare. In the 1968 and 1969 budgets we were able to increase the staff by 15 officers which allowed the police to provide the service we had strived so hard to develop since 1964.

The population in 1968 had reached 56,472 and the police officers had increased to 47 which reduced the ratio to one to 1,200.

The public at large has to realize that to give service 24 hours per day, seven days per week requires a minimum of five officers to field one platoon per shift. With four platoons it would require 20 officers per day to man the service as a week has seven days times three eight hour shifts. The need to cover 21 shifts in a 7 day week would require eight more platoon officers for a total of 28. The need to cover court duty, annual leave, compensation leave, illness, etc., would add one officer per day. This adds up to 35 officers to man the front line. The additional 12 officers from the 47 available, would be involved in administration, special branch services and programs, Identification Branch Officers, and School Patrol Officers, training leave, etc. This accounted for the 47 officers on staff. It truly was a remarkably thin blue line.

Even with the number of officers on staff we were able to maintain our crime rate well below average, compared to municipalities with a similar population count, and at the same time we maintained a higher crime solving rate.

As we entered 1968 we experienced a rapid increase in the use of drugs. Marijuana increased by 400% alone plus other narcotics. This meant that we had serious additional problems developing in our communities across Canada and we too were not immune.

The Nepean Police believed that specialized training was essential for doing their job well. Every effort had been made through the years to continue to provide knowledge from attending the Ontario Police College with additional in-house programs. It has been one of our greatest assets.

NEPEAN POLICE GRADUATION—Reeve Aubrey Moodie, chairman of the Nepean Police Commission, congratulates four of the 15 police graduates who received certificates Friday in the council chambers. From left: Reeve Moodie and constables David Forbes, Clifford Bastien, Stewart Arnott and Devlon Fermoyle. (Journal Photo: Dominion Wide)

Nepean Township Police Firearms Programme recently completed shows Officers under direction of Cpl. N. Parks receiving Team Trophy from Louis (Jack) Trembley, Local Public Relations Officer of O'Keefe Brewing Company. From left to right: Cst. F. Gardner; Cst. J. Wilkinson; Cpl. N. Parks; Cst. J. Collins; Cst. S. Gilders; Absent Cst. W. Story.

ROYAL CANADIAN MOUNTED POLICE
BASIC FIELD IDENTIFICATION COURSE NO. 1
From November 2, 1964 to November 6, 1964
Back Row: D/Sgt. R. Duquette, Hull PD.; Cst. L. Moir, Gloucester P.D.; Capt. R. Knight, Gatineau P.D.;
Cpl. W. Brown, Gloucester P.D.; Sgt. G. Wersch, Nepean P.D.; Det. D. Cadieux, South Hull P.D.; Cst.
L. Cadieux, Aylmer P.D.
Front Row: Cst. R. Sincennes, Point Gatineau P.D.; Det. R. Dussault, Point Gatineau P.D.; Insp. W.M.
Harasym, Ass't Officer I/C Ident. Branch; Sgt E. Cuillerier, Hawkesbury P.D.; Cst. P. Page, Eastview P.D.

Field Identification Course graduates at RCMP College

The officers in the above photograph came from Nepean, Gloucester, Ottawa and the Quebec area adjoining Ottawa.

This was a special four day course on Basic Field Identification Techniques at the R.C.M.P. Ottawa.

The purpose was to assist officers who were directly involved at the scenes of crime and supervisors who would extend this information to the field officers. Nepean was represented by Sgt. E.Gus Wersch.

CHRISTMAS PARTY FOR SAFETY PATROLS—More than 400 public and separate school safety patrols were entertained at a four hour Christmas party Saturday at Merivale High School. Among those attending the party were, from left, Karen Maiden, Cost. John Wilkinson, Safety Officer, Cathy Hubley, Nepean Police Chief E.G. "Gus" Wersch and Julie Tubman.

Nepean Police "Razorbacks" Baseball Team.

The officers of the Nepean Township were very involved in community projects.

Community Services Handbook

Cst. Monica Hall

Nepean Township Police – Annual Firearms Trophy Winners from left to right: Cst. C. Raganold; Cst. T. Collins; Cpl. B. Easey; Mr. Jack Tremblay, Representative O'Keefe Breweries making the presentation; Cst. W. Taylor; Sgt. R. Elstone, Capt.; Cst. J. Wilkinson and Cst. W. Phillips. Cst. W. Phillips also won the Individual High Trophy.

Firearm Training Trophy Winners

A new weekly information program was developed called " You and The Law" in conjunction with the Nepean Clarion management as a community service.

This program was to inform the public of new by-laws that were passed, problem areas, increase of a particular criminal activities in a timely fashion.

The information was published from the Chief of Police Office. This information was well accepted from the feedback we received.

Another Train Motor Vehicle Collision

Nov. 9th, 1968 another train-motor vehicle collision, this time at the CNR crossing on Cedarview Road. Two people were killed from the motor vehicle. Two brothers were traveling in a Jeep station wagon which was totally demolished into small pieces of metal.

The CNR line with the level railway road crossing had been a major concern and frustration. It was impossible to curb and was dependent on the motor vehicle driver to watch for oncoming trains and slow down so that the vehicle could stop in time.

There was a great urgency to have Cedarview Road closed off and traffic diverted to an overpass at number 15 highway due to the heavy usage by both the CNR train and motor vehicles.

Drownings Increase

Other tragedies in 1968 showed an increase in drowning mishaps in pools, such as two young boys who along with five other playmates entered the public fenced in swimming pool at General Burns. They had been able to crawl through under the fence and two of them aged three and four fell in and drowned. Several other adult drowning cases were reported; in some cases alcohol use was a factor.

Another first for Nepean Police

Uniforms took on a new look in 1968. The Nepean Police were the first to wear a properly identified blue shirt in the hot summer months. The heavy dark blue serge was too hot, especially when the patrol cars did not have air conditioning. Some senior area police officers didn't agree, but within six months everyone wore uniform shirts in the warm summer weather.

January 1969 started off with another train motor vehicle collision, this time at the McFarlane Merivale road crossing. The driver escaped but his vehicle was demolished.

A new program was initiated in the greater police area called " Police Week." The police forces would join together and hold a one week presentation at a central area like the Ottawa Civic Centre and major malls. Each police department would set up displays and have officers attend to meet with the general public, free of charge.

This was an occasion to meet the officers and discuss different situations and be given special information pamphlets. Several patrol cars were on display for the children and adults alike to sit in a fully equipped police cruiser.

This became a popular annual project.

Representatives of the Seven Participating Ottawa Area Police Departments

YOU

and the

POLICE

Chief J. A. Cavan, K.M.
Ottawa Police Force

S/Sgt. A. H. Barker
Ontario Prov. Police

Chief K. Duncan
Gloucester
Police Force

Chief E. Saumure
Richmond
Police Force

Chief E. G. Wersch
Nepean
Police Force

Chief E. Claude Dwyer
Vanier
Police Force

Comm. W. L. Higgitt
R.C.M.P.

Area Chiefs of Police sponsoring the 1970 Police Week

The Police Week project was developed by the area Police Forces to meet the public in a casual non-structured way at different locations each year in the month of May.

Nepean Police - Police Week Display at Bayshore.

Patrol car 1965 with Sgt E. Gus Wersch and Constable Peter Monette.

Constable John Wilkinson's Safety Cruiser – A popular Patrol vehicle used for the School Patrol program.

Nepean Township Police Winning team for the Annual Firearms Training and Competition Trophy – presented by Mr. Fern Groleau, representative of O'Keefe Breweries. From left to right: Ray Sabourin, G. Knox, Cpl. N. Parks (Captain), Paul Charlebois, Mr. Groleau, G. Deavy, and S. Gilders.

NEPEAN TOWNSHIP
POLICE DEPARTMENT
1965

Cst. Larry McCourt earned top Marks in the firearm training program.

A change in the school program was in replacing Cst. John Wilkinson to allow him to be involved with other areas of the police service. His work with the school safety and patrol area was greatly appreciated for a job well done.

Cst. William Taylor became an icon in the community and was highly praised and respected. His work with the school safety branch will be remembered as a true hero by all the school crossing guards he trained and by his relentless hands on safety teaching.

School patrollers visiting Government House with Her Excellency Lilly Schreyer in May 1980

School Patrollers Chief of Police for the Day.

School patrollers were awarded a "T" shirt and a visit to the Chief of Police Office where they received a certificate and were inducted as the Chief of Police and toured the Nepean Police Station wearing the Chief's Cap.

St. Joseph Training School Program

The Nepean Township Police were involved with an annual visit, co-sponsored with the Eastern Ontario Police Departments. Each of the larger police forces that participated would take a turn to be the host police department.

Members of the police would be introduced to the student body and then would participate and judge sports events for the day, followed by a dinner, where prizes were presented for the winners of the events. This was an opportunity to mingle with the students.

St. Joseph Training School was established for wayward teenagers to be rehabilitated. It was considered a very successful program and the annual police visit was a welcome occasion for both the police officers and the students who came from the communities where the police officers worked.

How they compare

1970 Report.

Municipality	Reported crimes	No. cleared*	Approx. per cent clear
Ottawa	22,316	3,856	17
Hull	4,229	691	17
Nepean	2,082	524	25
Gloucester	1,321	692	48
Gatineau	557	104	18
Pte. Gatineau	733	122	16
Vanier	1,637	495	30
Touraine	230	178	78
Templeton	126	108	85
Deschenes	20	8	40
Rockcliffe Park (OPP detachment)	126	40	30

*A crime is accounted "cleared" either when a charge is laid or when police have sufficient information but cannot lay a charge for various reasons.

The above shows a comparison of how the Nepean Police related to the greater Ottawa area.

As we continued our sojourn through the early 1970's the police continued to be visible with community programs. They provided the field police security patrols, investigate motor vehicle collisions, criminal and domestic occurrences in an attempt to maintain a high level of law and order.

Continuation of the Nepean Police Involvement in Activities Through the 1970's

On Dec 24th, 1971, an armed bank robbery occurred at the Bayshore Shopping Centre. Investigation resulted in conducting a raid at a residence. The suspects were arrested and charged.

Another train motor vehicle collision at the Woodroffe Ave. crossing took the life of the female driver of the motor vehicle. This had been a major concern since 1964. There was an urgent need for an overpass as too many lives had been lost.

The 1972 statistics for the greater Ottawa area showed an alarming rate in the narcotic cases as compared to 1970 which had 6,745 cases reported and investigated, in 1972 the increase went to 10,137 cases.

The most common drug cases were related to marijuana and hashish use.

The Nepean Township Police patrol car's new logo and design. March 1972 Could this be the real Batmobile?

Nepean Township Logo

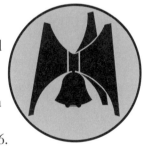

The new Nepean Township Police patrol vehicles had white doors, dropped the word Township, and added the bell logo. The bell had been rescued from the Nepean Township Hall in Westboro and installed in a special designed stand in front of the new Township Hall at 3825 Richmond Road in Bells Corners in 1966.

The stand had three height levels with the Bell hanging from underneath at its centre.

The design used on the Nepean Township logo was described earlier in this history as representing the family community.

The three heights of the holding stand represent a community family; father, mother and child. The bell referenced the history of a prominent Nepean family as far back as 1896 when it was installed at the Westboro Nepean Township Hall.

When the Nepean Police used the design as a logo on its police patrol vehicles, it in many ways resembled the batmobile logo. As the patrol cars travelled the different areas of Nepean and elsewhere they were referred to as the Nepean Police Batmobile, especially by the younger generation, which turned out to be good public relations as fighting for the rights of the people.

The Nepean Township population continued to increase at a rapid pace. In 1964 there were 35,266 residents, by 1972 the population had increased 65,932, almost doubling in eight years.

The Nepean Police had to increase at a reasonable level from 20 officers and two civilians in 1964 to 65 officers and nine civilians in 1972, still at the low end of the scale in police to population ratio of 1 to 1,034.

A common excuse was that we had a younger aged population who were not involved in criminal activities along with the cost to hire police officers and maintenance related to salary, equipment, vehicles, etc.

The Nepean Police took the position that we made a great effort to provide the community programs to maintain a positive prevention attitude which paid off in the long run, but they were also costly in manpower. Our prevention programs exceeded the costs by providing a healthier and safer place to live for the families who were raising their children which was evident by the population explosion.

The thinking also failed to realize that we, as a growing municipality, were in the corridor of three major centres, Toronto, Ottawa-Hull, and Montreal where the crime rate had been high, and that criminals from these areas were able to access Nepean within a few hours or minutes from the local area level.

The criminal element were always looking to establish themselves in new growing areas where they were not known and where some commercial enterprises were easy prey.

Ninety percent of our serious crimes were committed by outsiders which proved the point.

As we headed into 1973 an increase in snowmobile fatalities were reported and investigated along with drowning cases.

Newspaper of the day headlines reported that six snowmobile fatalities occurred in the greater Ottawa area within two weeks. They called it a snowmobile carnage.

The Nepean Police had purchased a snowmobile and trailer, a well equipped rescue boat with a trailer, and two motorcycle dirt bikes to be equipped to deal with the investigations that may occur at any moment's notice.

We had a well trained underwater rescue squad to patrol the Ottawa and Rideau Rivers that bordered Nepean Township. The officers were fully trained with certificates such as underwater scuba diving and as a boating rescue response team.

Constable Paul Delahay headed the team with Sergeant Ron Driscoll, Constable Les Frost, Constable Paul Bullied, Constable Gerry Trudel Constable Bev Mercier and Constable Brad Spriggs. Some of their training was done on their own time as a contribution to the community.

Constable Paul Delahay was in charge of the Under Water and Rescue Squad and brought the water safety concerns to the residents by a demonstration that the use of a fully inflated spare tire with the tire rim would support three adult persons by keeping them afloat. Its amazing why this life saving device hasn't been considered by the general public at beaches and boating areas. The vehicles in nearby parking lots had spare tires that could be readily available.

A full page of the demonstration with photographs in the Nepean Clarion brought this to the attention of the readers in the surrounding communities. Many letters were received from residents thanking the Nepean Police for bringing this life saving information to them.

Cst. Bev Mercier and Cst. Stu Arnott with Police Patrol and Rescue Boat.

How many times do we see headlines in lur newspapers - "youth drowns" as friends were unable to go to his assistance because they couldn't swim or someone drowns attempting to save a swimmer in difficulties - Are these tragedies necessary?

Hundreds of automobiles are usually parked at beaches or in the vicinity of other recreational water areas - each one of these vehicles generally has a spare tire and if inflated can become an emergency life preserver, not only for the swimmer in trouble but also for the rescuer.

The Nepean Police Force, Underwater Diving Rescue Squad under direction of Constable Paul Delahay conducted tests recently - using a spare tire from a 1973 Ford which was a radial tire size 825 x 15 - fully inflated and mounted on a rim.

The following photographs show that the spare tire when inflated, mounted on a rim will float and support at least four average sized adults - in an emergency the spare tire can become a life preserver.

The spare tire can be used in an emergency in the winter months as well. We have seen headlines whereby a person has fallen into open water or broken through ice, once again the spare tire can

No. 3
Cst. Paul Delahay, Cst. P. Bullied and Cpl. Driscoll supported by a spare tire.

No. 4 Cst. Delahay, Bullied, Frost and Cpl. Driscoll supported by a spare tire.

No. 7 Cst. Paul Delahay pulling Cst. L. Frost to safety using a spare tire

be used in an emergency such as this to assist the person in distress.

In this article, it is not suggested that all the rules of warer safety and other precautions should be abandoned. indeed, a continued emphasis should be placed on these safety rules. The use of the spare tire is advocated only in emergency situations. to bring to the puonc's attention that there is a device available which in some instances could be the difference between life and death.

No. 8
Cst. Paul Delahay towing Cst. L. Frost to safety being supported by a spare tire.

Glen Cairn Culvert Drowning

Rescue comes too late to save boy in culvert

By Bob Marleau
Citizen staff writer

A five-year-old Hazeldean boy died in hospital Friday three hours after being rescued by police divers from an underground culvert.

Timothy Joseph Stevens had been trapped in 2½ feet of water for three hours.

The boy, who lived at 29 Sheldrake Dr., had been standing on the culvert behind his home when the snow gave way beneath his feet, dropping him onto a thin layer of ice at the opening of the culvert.

Other children watched horror stricken as Timothy crashed through the ice and disappeared into the culvert's four foot opening.

The boy's seven-year-old brother jumped into the water but was unable to reach Timothy before he was swept out of sight.

Nepean police divers arrived on the scene shortly after the 4:24 p.m. accident and struggled through silt and debris for three hours before being able to reach the boy. Ron a Les Frost

Police said Timothy was swept 700 feet through the underground water passage before a build-up of debris blocked the tunnel just 200 feet from the exit. The culvert runs under a soccer field.

While firemen tried unsuccessfully to clear stumps jammed at the opposite end of the culvert, the two divers worked their way from the opening where the boy had fallen in.

"The divers did not have enough headroom to get through because of the silt at the bottom," said OPP Constable Richard Lacey, the investigating officer.

Police said the unconscious boy was transferred to the Children's Hospital of Eastern Ontario after doctors at the Queensway-Carleton Hospital examined him.

The boy never regained consciousness and at 10:25 p.m. was pronounced dead by coroner John Dickson. It is not known yet if an inquest will be held.

The boy is the child of Geraldine and Robert Stevens.

—Jim Merrithew, Citizen
Goulbourn culvert where Timmy Stevens died

February 23, 1978

C/Sgt. R. Driscoll
Nepean Police Force
3825 Richmond Rd.
Ottawa, Ontario.

Dear Sergeant Driscoll:

      The Board of Commissioners of Police for the Township
of Nepean has been appraised of the details surrounding the tragedy
involving Timothy Joseph Stevens of Glen Cairn in the Township of
Goulbourn.

      Your participation as a member of the Nepean Police Under-
water and Rescue Squad in the recovery of the victim showed extreme
courage and devotion to duty.

      The Board extends their appreciation for service beyond
the call of duty by presenting this citation to you on behalf of
the Nepean Police Commission and residents of Nepean.

      Congratulations and best wishes.

          Yours truly,

          A. S. Haydon
          Chairman

Two members of the Nepean Police under water diving squad responded to the assistance of the Ontario Provincial Police. A five year old boy had fallen into an open ditch filled with a high level of fast flowing water leading to a 3.5 foot culvert. The water only having about eight inch clearance at the top.

The two Nepean Police Officers, Sgt. Ron Driscoll and Constable Les Frost with their diving gear floated themselves feet forward into the tunnel fastened to ropes maintained by the Nepean Fire Department. At a distance of approximately 500 feet they came upon a log jam, with the young boy caught by the debris.

The boy was removed but due to the time between the report and the rescue, it was too late to revive the victim. Needless to say, it was unfortunate that the life of the boy could not be saved. The action by the two officers with the assistance of the Fire Department relieved the anxiety of the parents and the community. This action took courage and devotion to duty as well as a great risk to their own lives.

Their efforts were heartily applauded. It proved that the Under Water Squad was a necessary part of the Nepean Police Organization.

The dirt bike used by officers were to patrol lands of the greenbelt within Nepean to curb property damage and general trespassing.

Many calls had been received that motor cycle riders were using abandoned quarries to have drug and

Dirt bikes for NCC Patrol Cst. Jeff Patterson and Cst. Hadden Smith

drinking parties, especially on weekends. With regular patrols we were able to curb these activities.

The Dirt Bikes were also used for searches in the open land and bush area of the NCC greenbelt.

Snowmobile for search and Rescue

Bayshore Shopping Centre Opens, Largest in Area

On August the 8th, 1973 the largest area shopping centre opened at Bayshore Drive in Nepean, by Cambridge Leaseholds Limited. It contained several floors with104 indoor shopping businesses and center courts in the 695,000 square foot centre. The management predicted that 25,000 shoppers per day by year end would attend the centre.

This obviously brought with it a motor vehicle traffic concerns, as well as criminal activity such as shoplifting and armed robberies. It required a continuing presence by the Nepean Police as it was a community within itself.

1974 was a continuation of providing police services to the community. The general police presence and patrols were effective to keep traffic and criminal activities in check.

Again, motor vehicle collisions and drowning cases were responsible for a number of lives. In these mishaps, sad to say most of them were preventable.

We continued to work with the local newspaper, the Nepean Clarion, to provide information on different policing issues on a timely, weekly basis to the residents of Nepean. This was a highly successful program.

Our "You and the Law" publications, explaining new laws that had been legislated provided information to keep our residents informed was well received.

First Murder Investigation for the Nepean Township Police, September 26th, 1975

We were able to effectively cope with a number of serious crimes against persons and property, but none brought home the benefits of our training programs, such as a call on a Friday afternoon, in 1975. Several hours after school was out for the day, we received a report that an eight year old girl was missing from a public school in Barrhaven and did not come home as usual.

The Criminal Investigation Officers responded and covered the immediate area and were able to establish that the girl was last seen being called to a car by a male person to help him with some books at the front of the public school. He was allegedly delivering to the school around 2:30 p.m. No one saw the girl after that.

This triggered a major search throughout the night gradually extending out to the rural area as a number of farms had old unused buildings on them. By

11:00 a.m. on Saturday morning, while officers were searching one of the old abandoned barns, tire marks were noticed in the soft ground. A farmer stated he had seen a dark car near the barn in the late afternoon the day before, Friday.

A thorough search of the hayloft showed some recently disturbed hay. When the hay was removed it revealed the body of the missing girl. The girl had been raped and then shot with a four-ten shotgun through her chest. Sgt. Robert Mancuso found the slain girl. It was heartbreaker for the officers who were involved in the search.

From a composite drawing of the suspect made with the assistance of a specialist from the RCMP as described by witnesses was immediately distributed by the Nepean investigating officers to other area police resulted in the recognition by an Ottawa police officer who thought it may be a person who he had recent dealings with, for which he had an address in the City of Ottawa.

An immediate search warrant was obtained and the suspect was arrested as well as finding a four-ten shotgun wrapped in a jute bag under his bed, which proved to be the weapon used to kill the girl.

We had been put to our ultimate test and succeeded, within 24 hours from the report of the abduction the body was found, within 48 hours the suspect was arrested. The alarm of a child kidnapper being in the area was removed from the community before school classes opened on Monday. It was a tremendous relief.

The suspect was convicted and sentenced to life imprisonment. He died a few years later in prison.

The community responded by showing their personal feelings by sending letters to the local area newspapers.

"Your staff handled themselves in a most professional, efficient and effective manner; one which makes the residents extremely proud and the envy of police forces in the area."

Thanks were expressed to the officer of the Ottawa Police and for the composite drawing of the suspect, which helped us to resolve this heinous crime.

This was a classic case where the training programs, especially the Criminal Investigation, gave the officers of the Nepean Police the expertise in being able to handle cases at this level.

His Royal Highness Prince Charles Visits Nepean April 25th, 1975

Prince Charles on a visit to the City of Ottawa took an extended tour to visit the Nepean Township Sportsplex, a new facility that was considered a model development where all facets of sports were able to be played and provide facilities for indoor and outdoor major competitions.

The Nepean Police assisted in the security for this, being the first Royal Visit to Nepean.

New Nepean Police Accommodation

New Nepean Police accommodation had been in the planning stages and early in 1977, after a hearing by the Ontario Municipal Board, the building of a stand alone Police Station to be located at 245 Greenbank Road was approved to proceed. The location placed the building in the center of the built up area with easy access to all areas of the community. The Nepean Police Force by now had a staff of 100 police officers and 26 civilians for a total complement of 126 persons.

Training Highlights

Ninety one officers received training from a one day refresher course to a three week orientation to police duties for recruits provided by the Nepean Police Training Officer. These training courses were followed up by three months in field experience with a senior officer, after which, the recruits were sent on a six week course at the Ontario Police College in Aylmer, Ontario.

The population had escalated to 78,602 by the end of 1977. The police ratio dropped to one to 786 residents.

A Unique Murder Case of a Drowning in a Bathtub Scenario

On July 6th 1978, Frederick George Ruddick, who always professed his innocence, was convicted of First Degree Murder, for the drowning of his wife in a bathtub. He was sentenced to life imprisonment.

When Justice J. O'Driscoll gave his charge to the jury he stated, "Fred Ruddick did kill his wife he was a crafty, cunning killer who almost pulled off the perfect crime".

This case was the classic example of the perfect crime clashing with the perfect investigation.

Crown Attorneys M.A.F. Lindsay and Andrejs Berzins summed up the case with their following conclusion in a letter addressed to Chief Gus Wersch of the Nepean Police.

"….. The success of this prosecution was largely due to the hard work of members of your police department and we are very much indebted to your force.

We would like to make particular mention of Sergeant Robert Mancuso and Det. Murray Gordon, who devoted so much of their time and energy to the investigation and to the preparation of the case for trial.

You are well aware that they worked many long hours, often days in a row, to put together this complicated case.

They made themselves available to us at all hours of the day, never complaining about the hardships that must have fallen on themselves and their family.

We sincerely feel that their determination carried the day as far as the outcome of the case is concerned and we were particularly pleased with their good humor at all times, even under stress.

Thank you Nepean, you are guaranteed to reap the dividends…."

(In the presentation of this case to the jury, a complete detailed reconstruction of the bathroom was built and made available to the Court along with many other items considered evidence.)

Other Nepean Police Officers from the Detective Division and the Identification Branch played a major role as the case was being investigated to support the lead investigators.

Since the trial all appeals were denied.

Nepean Police Centre Opened and Nepean is Elevated to City Status

The official opening took place on November 29th 1978, which followed a day after the Nepean Township was granted city status. From this day forward Nepean would be officially called the City of Nepean.

Our next major move forward was in November 1978, when we moved into the new police facilities, (we finally came out from the basement) which was classed as the most modern police station in Canada.

Nepean City Police Centre Officially opened November 29th, 1978 located at 245 Greenbank Road, Nepean, just as the Nepean Township changed its status to the City of Nepean.

Looking forward

Spring of 1979......

Bears repeating...

Nepean City Police Centre, 1978. Located at 245 Greenbank Road, Nepean Ontario well centered in the heart of the populated area, with easy access to all parts of the City.

Nepean Population Growth

By the time the Municipality received city status, the population had grown from 35,266 in 1964 to 80,506 in 1978 and the staff on the Nepean Police grew accordingly to a staff of 102 officers and 21 civilians.

With the new facilities we were able to move forward by installing our automated records system as well as increasing our field capabilities by establishing a Firearms Branch, Drug Investigation Unit, Crime Prevention, Property Control and a special Transport Branch. We were fast becoming the envy of Police Services across Canada and had visitors from New Brunswick to Vancouver to see our station. These were proud moments for the force.

The plaque at the main entrance has a special story, in that when the plaque was installed it had a surname spelled wrong and had to be removed with the inscription to be repeated on what was originally the back, then reinstalled. This meant that the plaque has two inscriptions front and back, however the back is now embedded in mortar.

The Inscription on Plaque

The plaque lists the date of the Official Opening, with the name of the person doing the honours of the event.

Sidney Handleman M.P.P. Carleton

Names of the Nepean City Council of the day.

Names of the Nepean Police Commissioners.

Chief of Police ...............................E.G. Wersch

The Architect ....Hans L. Stutz

The Contracting firm...W.M. Construction Ltd.

Plaque embedded in wall of the main entrance lobby of the Nepean Police Centre.

Official Party waiting in the Chief's boardroom before opening ceremony November 29th, 1978. Waiting for Mr. Sydney Handleman M.P.P. to arrive.

The Premier of the Province of Ontario was scheduled to be the Official representative to lead the opening ceremony, however due to some emergent commitment he was unable to be present.

The local Member of Parliament Sydney Handleman M.P.P. was called on to perform the official duties on behalf of the Province of Ontario.

Opening ceremonies November 28, 1978: Chief Gus Wersch, Mayor A. Haydon, Councillor B. Franklin, Walter Baker, M. P.

Sydney Handleman M.P.P. and the Honorable Walter Baker on tour at the new police centre.

Honorable Walter Baker MP passing Canadian flag to Chief Gus Wersch at the opening ceremonies of the Nepean Police Centre, 1978. The Flag would be flown from the mast at the front of the Police Centre, 245 Greenbank, Road, Nepean, Ontario.

Chief Gus Wersch discusses facilities of New Police Centre with Grant Carman, Nepean Council Member.

The old Dispatch Centre 1966-1978 Constable Robin Easey and Constable Don Graves. At 3825 Richmond Road, Bells Corners.

Ron Meyer, President of Versaterm presenting Chief Gus Wersch with a plaque for pioneering the development of computer based records systems that was installed in the new Nepean Police Centre, the products of which were adopted by many police forces throughout Canada and the United States.

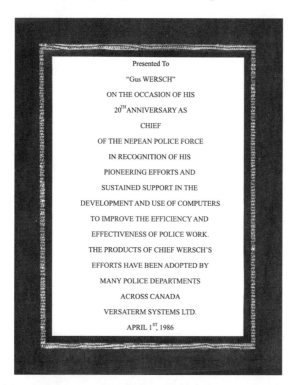

Presented To

"Gus WERSCH"

ON THE OCCASION OF HIS

20[TH]ANNIVERSARY AS

CHIEF

OF THE NEPEAN POLICE FORCE

IN RECOGNITION OF HIS

PIONEERING EFFORTS AND

SUSTAINED SUPPORT IN THE

DEVELOPMENT AND USE OF COMPUTERS

TO IMPROVE THE EFFICIENCY AND

EFFECTIVENESS OF POLICE WORK.

THE PRODUCTS OF CHIEF WERSCH'S

EFFORTS HAVE BEEN ADOPTED BY

MANY POLICE DEPARTMENTS

ACROSS CANADA

VERSATERM SYSTEMS LTD.

APRIL 1ST, 1986

Plaque with inscription presented to Chief Wersch by Pres. Ron Meyer of Versaterm Ltd.

Constable T. O'Donovan assisted by civilian Don Sproule

Modern Communications Centre with all the latest technology available, it even included a special telephone for the hard of hearing residents to communicate directly by a telephone telex system.

Nepean Police control centre, dispatch console – showing the first line technology equipment available at the time.

All the wiring was hidden in a 12 inch space under the floating tiled floor, as each 2 foot square tile could be individually lifted to access the wiring and telephone incoming lines.

Photos of the Nepean Police Communication Centre installed in the Nepean Police Centre at 245 Greenbank Road in 1978.

CHAPTER 7: NEPEAN POLICE FORCE

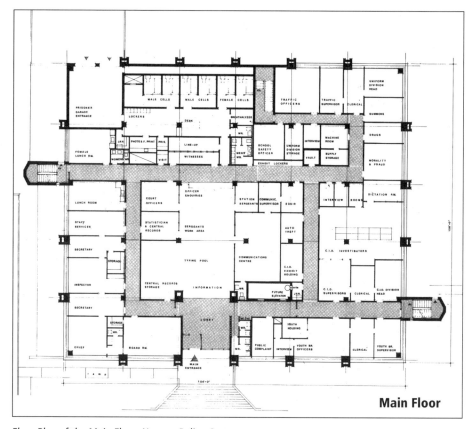

Floor Plan of the Main Floor, Nepean Police Centre

On November 29th, 1978 the Hon. Sidney Handleman officially opened the Nepean Police Centre.

Our new quarters are now centrally located at 245 Greenbank Road.

We are extremely proud of our new accommodations and can now boast one of the finest Police Buildings in Canada.

The highlights of the facilities are outlined as follows:

Main Floor

The Main Floor has a gross area of 19,150 square feet. The Public entrance faces west and is accessible from Greenbank Road.

Immediately accessible from the lobby is the information desk and the record retrieval area. The records section and adjoining communications centre form the central core of the structure, from which the numerous bureaus within the Police Force radiate.

The specially designed console in the Communications Branch contains built-in radio and telephonic communication systems, controls for the closed circuit TV system, security door controls and an illuminated status map. The security areas and entrances may be monitored from this console using the closed circuit TV system.

Surrounding this core are the various offices including the Administration Wing, Board Room, Youth Branch, Criminal Investigation Division, Uniform Division, Traffic Branch and School Safety Officer.

The security area includes a drive-in garage, male and female holding cells, interview area, fingerprint room, breathalyzer room, as well as witness and identification rooms, making it a secure and efficient receiving area.

Ground Floor

The centre of the Ground Floor is comprised of a combined Training Room/Lecture Room which is divided by a sound-proof partition. The entire area may be used for large scale meetings or as an emergency control centre. The exercise room adjacent to the meeting hall, will be equipped to permit the development of a physical culture program.

The ground floor also contains a modern Identification Branch complete with necessary laboratory facilities; such as a film room, paper room, fingerprint room, drafting equipment and exhibit examination areas.

The Field Supervisor's office is located directly across the hall, which houses portable radios and other emergency equipment which are issued to officers for field use. A report room is located next to the briefing room where the officers can write, dictate and/or type their reports. The Training Officer is conveniently located in this area, with accommodation for clerical staff and a library which will be used for research and educational purposes.

Second Floor

The remainder of the second floor houses, locker rooms, lunch rooms, stolen goods storage, workshop, identification garage, and a firearms training indoor range with the air controls to remove all contamination, with firing points at 15-20 and 25 yard distances.

As the officers enter the rear of the station at ground level, they have their locker rooms, a wet coat drying room, with a muster room to assemble for briefing sessions before going out on patrol.

Communications

"...the hub of the forces activities..."

The daily operation of any police force is gauged by the efficiency and effectiveness of its communication system —our force is no exception. The ability to position police officers at the right place and time gives better police protection to citizens, helps to increase the possibility of apprehension and often reduces the seriousness of the offense.

The new communications centre contains some of the most modern facilities available. The specially designed single or two man console contains a built in radio and telephone communications systems, controls for the closed circuit TV, security door controls and an illuminated status map. The console also contains a computer terminal (C.P.I.C.), as well as the vehicle fuel control system. The security areas and entrances are monitored from this console using the closed circuit TV system. There are ten incoming telephone lines, each line automatically tape recorded. The recorded telephone as well as the radio communications to mobile units have the capabilities of instant replay.

A giant step forward in an area which controls the pulse of the entire operation.

The communication centre described above is certainly a top of the line facility, providing the officers and staff with an area that is secure, with equipment to respond to all emergencies.

The main floor houses the administration offices, which accommodates the Office of the Chief of Police, within a secure area, but available to members of the public by appointment.

The area adjoining the Chief's Office has a board room for meetings with members of the community as required and in house meetings with senior officers.

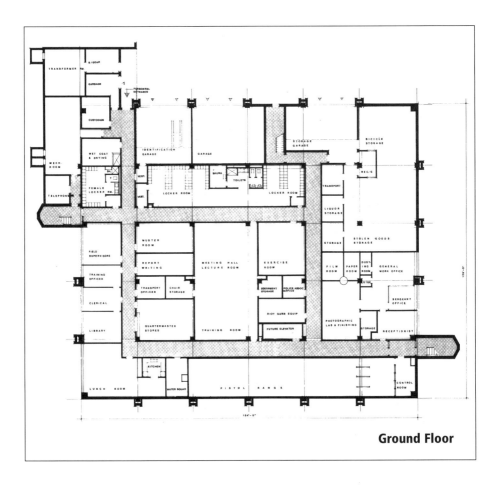

Ground Floor

THE POLICE EXEMPLARY SERVICE MEDAL

has been awarded to

E.G. WERSCH

in recognition of twenty years of loyal and meritorious service to law enforcement in Canada.

Ed Schreyer

Governor General of Canada

Police Service Medal

Issued for 20 years service, the bar on the Ribbon with two stars denotes 30 years of service.

Each star on the bar represents an additional five years service.

A certificate is issued in the recipient's name signed by the Governor General of Canada

Mess Kit Medal and Regular Medal

Police Service Medal issued for 20 Years, then a star on bar for every five years additional service.

The Police patrol car had a new look, with all the equipment necessary to do an effective job in the field, portable radios were a major addition to the Patrol Officers, in situations when leaving the patrol vehicle they still had instant communication with Station or other officers in their vicinity.

Moving forward...

Photo of Patrol Car in the late 1970 and 1980's

Design on Early Edition Patrol Cars 1964

Nepean Police Patrol Cars and Identification van

Mobile Field Identification Van.

Sgt Wayne Levere's Identification Team
Back Row: Sgt Wayne Levere, Cst. D. Wilson, Cst.Peter Richard, Cst. Les Frost, Cst. Tom Collins.
Front Row: Lynne Dirani, and Trish Lacroix.

Identification Branch – Nepean Police.

Nepean Identification Branch Staff under direction of Staff Sgt. Brian McGarvey (lower right).

The Identification Branch Officers and Staff are a crucial support group and have the responsibility to gather evidence at serious motor vehicle collisions and major crime scenes.

Their duties required them to put the evidence together for court presentations.

The new Nepean Police Centre at 245 Greenbank Road which opened in 1978 had an up to date facility equipped to accommodate the staff to provide the support necessary to the field investigation staff.

One of the major components of Identification Branch was the special area that enabled the staff to examine exhibits indoors by having the availability of a secure garage location that could be locked down so that exhibits would not be contaminated, a vital requirement for court presentations.

Nepean Police Cap Badge   *Shoulder Flash*

HISTORY OF EMBLEM USED ON
NEPEAN POLICE SHOULDER FLASH

The emblem on the shoulder flash was adopted by the Nepean Township Council on January 26, 1970 as the Township's Official Emblem.

The architectural structure supporting the bell has three supports, each of a different height. The tallest support represents the "father", the medium height support represents the "mother" and the shortest represents the "child". When conjoined they denote "family". Nepean Township is a progressive family community and it is only befitting that the emblem bears this out.

The bell in the emblem brings with it some history and heritage. It was hung in the old Township Hall at 345 Richmond Road in the area known as Westboro before 1950. The town hall itself was erected in 1896. The bell survived one fire and was used in the earlier days to ring out the daily curfew at 9:00 p.m. and also to call out the volunteer fire brigade.

In November 1966 upon the completion of the new Township Hall at Bells Corners, the bell was removed from the old building and set into its present position in the structure in front of the new hall. To remind us of the past, it was rung at the official opening of the new Township Hall.

YEAR	POPULATION	POLICE OFFICERS	CIVILIANS	TOTAL STRENGTH
1957	10,963	From 1957-63 a Joint Force - Gloucester		
1958	11,756	Nepean Police Force started with five		
1959	13,724	employees, one Chief of Police and four		
1960	16,566	Constables. The following is the staff		
1961	21,055	record which shows the growth from 1964		
1962	26,131	to 1982, when the Nepean Police Force was		
1963	30,446	established as a separate Force.		
1964	35,266	20	1	21
1965	40,811	24	1	25
1966	45,934	28	2	30
1967	49,701	32	7	39
1968	53,148	38	8	46
1969	56,572	49	5	54
1970	60,639	57	6	63
1971	66,000	60	9	69
1972	70,000	65	9	74
1973	74,000	72	11	83
1974	75,000	85	17	102
1975	76,000	94	18	112
1976	76,208	95	19	114
1977	78,602	101	19	120
1978	80,506	101	22	123
1979	82,000	101	25	126
1980	83,000	106	26	132
1981	84,500	111	27	138
1982	85,737	112	27	139

Population with staff growth from 1957 to 1982.

Nepean City Police Ceremonial Flag

The following pages will show the administration and operational structure with assigned divisions showing the organizational structure and responsibilities for the officer in charge of the division he is assigned to.

These excerpts are from the 1987 annual report, and had been the basic organizational structure since 1978 when we were able to define the police functions in the new police centre.

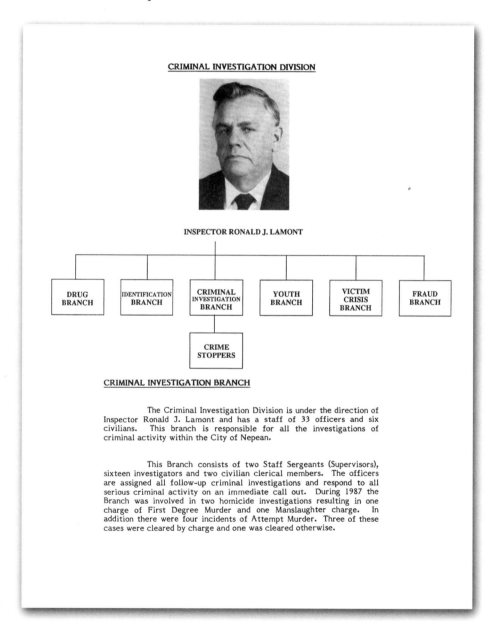

CRIMINAL INVESTIGATION DIVISION

INSPECTOR RONALD J. LAMONT

DRUG BRANCH | IDENTIFICATION BRANCH | CRIMINAL INVESTIGATION BRANCH | YOUTH BRANCH | VICTIM CRISIS BRANCH | FRAUD BRANCH

CRIME STOPPERS

CRIMINAL INVESTIGATION BRANCH

The Criminal Investigation Division is under the direction of Inspector Ronald J. Lamont and has a staff of 33 officers and six civilians. This branch is responsible for all the investigations of criminal activity within the City of Nepean.

This Branch consists of two Staff Sergeants (Supervisors), sixteen investigators and two civilian clerical members. The officers are assigned all follow-up criminal investigations and respond to all serious criminal activity on an immediate call out. During 1987 the Branch was involved in two homicide investigations resulting in one charge of First Degree Murder and one Manslaughter charge. In addition there were four incidents of Attempt Murder. Three of these cases were cleared by charge and one was cleared otherwise.

UNIFORM DIVISION

INSPECTOR DEVON FERMOYLE

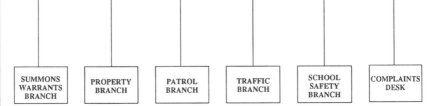

SUMMONS WARRANTS BRANCH	PROPERTY BRANCH	PATROL BRANCH	TRAFFIC BRANCH	SCHOOL SAFETY BRANCH	COMPLAINTS DESK

The Uniform Division is under the direction of Inspector Devon Fermoyle and has a staff of seventy six officers and six civilians.

PATROL BRANCH

The Patrol Branch is on a 10 1/4 hours peak policing shift schedule. This system is designed with eight platoons consisting of 1 patrol sergeant and seven constables. Our station staff sergeants are directly responsible for two platoons each, as well as being in charge of the police centre. Two platoons are deployed during the high crime and calls for service period, while one platoon is deployed during the low crime time. This system allows for increased response time, efficiency, adequate patrols and security for our residents.

The patrol officers are the front line of the police force. They are the first to respond to all calls for service within the City. Our patrol officers are trained to handle emergencies, surveillances, crime prevention strategies and general calls, they are expected to act as lawyer, judge, social worker, referee, friend and defender. There is no other profession that places such demands on their employees. Our men respond, evaluate and react to this challenge in a professional and efficient manner.

The officers of our patrol division have done a commendable job in many encounters with the citizens of our community and their initial contact sets the tone for resolving what they face.

STAFF SERVICES DIVISION

IINSPECTOR GORD DEAVY

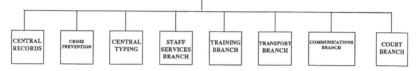

CENTRAL RECORDS	CRIME PREVENTION	CENTRAL TYPING	STAFF SERVICES BRANCH	TRAINING BRANCH	TRANSPORT BRANCH	COMMUNICATIONS BRANCH	COURT BRANCH

The Staff Services Division is under the direction of Inspector Gord Deavy which has a staff of nine officers and twenty-five civilians who are responsible for all the support services to the Force as a whole. The Branches and their responsibilities within this Division are as follows:

TRAINING BRANCH

One Sergeant and a civilian clerical member are assigned on a full time basis to this Branch. All the internal staff training, external training arrangements, dissemination of new Legislation, and maintenance of records related thereto are part of this Branch's activities. Other responsibilities include the operation of the Force Library, preparation of video training aids, and an extensive Firearms Training Program.

Good member selection does not void the need for training; it simply allows the Force to maximize the effectiveness of any training program which is given.

The criminal is no longer an amateur; the policeman must be his equal, whatever his speciality may be. Instruction must be continuous; knowledge must be updated frequently in such matters as the state of the law, aids to the police and current police matters.

The Summary of Training detailed on the following pages, exemplifies our objective.

Wayne Phillips, B.A.
Deputy Chief of Police

Field Operations

Field Operations is responsible for providing administrative co-ordination to the myriad of law enforcement activities that occur throughout the entire city. Working closely with the Chief of Police overall control and management of the Force is maintained.

The accomplishments of the Force are attributed to the loyal dedication of the Force members and the co-operative partnership forged with the citizens of Nepean. It is this teamwork we endeavor to maintain as we strive to enhance the quality of life we share in our City.

For the next five years, 1979 to 1982, the Nepean City Police, now well established in their new accommodation at 245 Greenbank Road, continued to develop the existing community programs and upgrade the training for the officers, especially in firearms.

The new facilities had a modern indoor firing range which allowed the training officer, to upgrade all the officers in house. A number of police departments in the smaller municipalities around the Ottawa area requested assistance to have their officers trained at the Nepean Police Firearms Range.

Constable Gary Meehan tests firing firearm.

NEPEAN POLICE FORCE
FIRST ANNUAL AWARDS DINNER
January 27, 1986

PROGRAM

1.	Welcome to Guests	Chief E. G. Wersch
2.	Grace	Insp. R. Elstone
3.	Toast to The Queen	Insp. R. Lamont
4.	Dinner	

5. **Presentations Announcements**   D/Chief W. Phillips

a) **20 Year Medals**
Cst. W. Mattingly
Cst. R. Gagne
Sgt. J. Wilkinson

Presented by Vice Chairman
Mayor B. Franklin and
Commissioner E. Gladu,
Nepean Police Commission

b) **30 Year Service Bars**
Insp. R. Elstone
S/Sgt. B. Easey

As above

c) **Citations for Bravery**
Cst. Robin Easey
Cst. Ralph Erfle

Presented by Chairman of
Board, Sid Handleman,
Nepean Police Commission

d) **Force Plaques for Bravery**
Cst. Robin Easey
Cst. Ralph Erfle

Presented by Chief Wersch

e) **Special Citation
to a Recipient**

Presented by Chief Wersch

f) **Citizen Citations**
Mr. Albert Burrell, Jr.
Miss Lynn Bronson
Mr. Louis Boulanger

Presented by Chief Wersch

g) **25 Year Gold Watch**
S/Sgt. R. Driscoll

Presented by S. Handleman,
Chairman of the Board

h) **Force Plaque**
To an Officer of the
Nepean Police Force

Presented by Insp. Devon
Fermoyle

i) **Appreciation Presentation**
His Honour Judge K. Flanigan

Presented by Vice Chairman
Mayor Ben Franklin and
Chief E.G. Wersch

6. **Remarks by Mayor Ben Franklin**

7. **Entertainment by Nepean Police Officers**

1)	S/Sgt. Bert & Gwen Easey	"Country Music & Songs"
2)	Cst. Ken Logan	"Recitals"
3)	Closing Pipe Recital	Cst. Lachlann Bisaillion "Amazing Grace"

8. **Closing Remarks**   Chief E. G. Wersch

1987 Civilian Office Staff

The civilian staff are an important extension of the field officers in the preparation of documents and reports for easy and quick reference, and maintaining the secure and confidential files.

Winners

Photos from Billboards of Nepean Police activities.

Insp. Ron Lamont, Chief Wersch, Sgt. Ron Driscoll Sgt. Wayne Levere

Nepean Police Curling Team entered at area Police Bonspiels.
Nepean Police Curling Bonspiel at Sportsplex.

The Nepean City Police Force rink received the Bank of Nova Scotia trophy after placing first in last Wednesday's Carleton Place Police Curling Bonspiel. From left to right is Peter Cuthbert, Katheryn Downie of the Bank of Nova Scotia, Ron Lamont, Police Chief Gus Wersch and Ron Driscoll.

Canadian Association of Chiefs of Police Photo at the Winnipeg, Manitoba Conference 1974
Front Row: Chief Gus Wersch, Nepean served as Sgt at Arms for three years, followed by seven years as Secretary Treasurer.

The Canadian Association of Chiefs of Police membership consisted of members from police forces throughout Canada. The governing body as shown above are elected by the membership at an annual conference, usually held and hosted at different cities throughout Canada.

The topics dealt with at these conferences related to concerns of existing laws that created problems with the enforcement by officers on the street and approving special recommendations and or presentations to the government of the day for changes to the legislated laws.

One of the highlights of the day off at the Halifax Conference was a trip on the famous Bluenose which will be remembered for years to come.

A day off at the Halifax Annual Conference in 1976.

The following pages will show the extent of the involvement by the Nepean City Police Officers as shown by the calls for service and comparison to previous years. (Taken from the Nepean City Police Annual Report for 1980.)

OCCURRENCES INVESTIGATED AS RECEIVED

Abduction	2
Alarms - Business	1,293
Alarms - Banks	82
Alarms - Residences	255
Alarms - Schools	54
Animal Bites	37
Animal Complaints	134
Animals to Pound	2
Arson	44
Assault - Common	107
Assault - Indecent	21
Assault - Causing Bodily Harm	22
Assistance to Other Police Forces	139
Auto Thefts	234
Auto Recovered	178
Bicycle Thefts	951
Bicycles Recovered	402
Bomb Scares	27
Break, Enter and Theft	925
Break & Enter Attempts	149
Break Outs	3
Compassion to Locate	39
Careless/Dangerous Drivers Reported	188
Counterfeit - Possession	0
Damage Wilful - Private Property	686
Damage Wilful - Public Property	116
Deaths	28
Disqualified Drivers	102
Disturbance - Causing Public	25
Disturbance - Domestic	257
Disturbance - General	345
Dogs	256
Drownings	1
Drugs - Overdose	6
Drugs - Seizure	103
Drunk Public Place	157
False Pretences	22
Fire	106
Firearms - Discharging	34
Firearms - Illegal Possession	3
Fraud	328
Harrassment	68
Indecent Exposure	61
Information Occurrences	24
Injured Persons	76
Impaired Drivers (Reported)	367

(Occurrences Investigated continued on the next page)

CRIMINAL STATISTICS (continued)

OCCURRENCES INVESTIGATED AS RECEIVED (continued)

```
Liquor Offences ........................................     529
Loitering .............................................       3
Mental Persons ........................................      75
Miscellaneous Complaints & Investigations ..............   2,178
Miscellaneous Traffic Complaints .......................   1,463
Mischief ..............................................     173
Missing Persons - Adults ..............................      30
Missing Persons - Children & Juveniles .................     201
Missing Persons - Adults Located .......................      29
Missing Persons - Children & Juveniles Located .........     197
Motor Vehicle Collisions ..............................   1,879
Murder - Attempts .....................................       3
Neighbour Disputes ....................................      22
Noise Complaints ......................................     573
Obscene - Letters .....................................       1
Obscene - Phone Calls .................................      40
Obstruct Police Officer ...............................      11
Parking Complaints ....................................     324
Phone Calls - Prank ...................................       6
Phone Calls - Harrassing ..............................      92
Phone Calls - Nuisance ................................       5
Phone Calls - Suspicious ..............................      37
Possession Stolen Property ............................      50
Property Reported Lost ................................     381
Property Reported Found ...............................     351
Prowlers ..............................................      68
Rape Reported .........................................       3
Recovered Stolen Property .............................      22
Request Police Officer ................................     552
Request Ambulance .....................................      12
Robbery With Violence .................................      14
Sick Persons ..........................................     124
Shoplifting ...........................................     423
Snowmobile Complaints .................................      27
Speeding - Complaints .................................      98
Suicide - Actual ......................................       7
Suspicious Auto .......................................     433
Suspicious Persons ....................................     568
Theft - Attempts ......................................     110
Theft - All Others ....................................   1,633
Threats - Letters .....................................       4
Threats - Phone Calls .................................      75
Threats - Verbal ......................................       7
Tours .................................................      70
Towed Vehicles ........................................      17
```

(Occurrences Investigated
continued on the next
page)

OCCURRENCES INVESTIGATED AS RECEIVED (continued)

```
Transportation by Fraud .................................      6
Trespassing - Petty Trespass Act .......................    156
Warrants - Arrest on ...................................    511
Warrants - Execution ...................................     64
Weapons - Dangerous ....................................     27
Weapons - Seizure ......................................      6
```

Total occurrences including Traffic Collisions and complaints investigated by the Nepean Police Force in 1980 were 22,149; this shows an increase of 826 or 3.8% over 1979.

OCCURRENCE COMPARISON DATA

YEAR	NUMBER OF OCCURRENCES	INCREASE/DECREASE OVER PREVIOUS YEAR
1971	13,187	increase over 1970 - 594 or 4.7%
1972	14,273	increase over 1971 - 1,086 or 8.2%
1973	14,685	increase over 1972 - 412 or 2.8%
1974	15,295	increase over 1973 - 610 or 4.2%
1975	15,037	decrease over 1974 - 258 or 1.7%
1976	15,480	increase over 1975 - 443 or 5.8%
1977	16,175	increase over 1976 - 695 or 4.5%
1978	20,443	increase over 1977 - 4,268 or 26.4%
1979	21,323	increase over 1978 - 880 or 4.3%
1980	22,149	increase over 1979 - 826 or 3.8%

Total Ten Year Increase .... 8,962 or 67.9%

NATURE OF OFFENCES	CHARGES LAID	DEFERRED ACTIONS
Arson	0	2
Assault (Bodily Harm)	2	4
Assault (Common)	6	11
Assault Police	0	1
Attempt Fraud	1	1
Attempt Theft	1	3
Break & Enter	2	4
Break, Enter & Mischief	2	0
Break, Enter & Theft	18	41
Break, Enter & Vandalism	0	2
Break, Enter with Intent	2	15
Carrying a Concealed Weapon	0	3
Causing a Disturbance	0	2
Counselling an Offence	0	1
Damage to Property	1	2
Dangerous Driving	0	1
Discharge Firearm	0	1
Drawing a Document without Authority ..	0	1
False Pretences	0	2
Fraud	0	2
Fraudulent use of Slugs	0	1
Harrassing Phone Calls	0	3
Harrassment	0	1
Mischief	13	24
Obstruct Police	0	2
Possession	17	25
Possession of Firearm	0	1
Public Mischief	2	2
Public Nudity	0	3
Robbery	2	0
Robbery with Threats of Violence	1	0
Setting Fires	0	2
Setting Fire by Negligence	0	2
Setting Fire to other Substances	0	1
Shoplifting	21	137
Take Auto Without Owners Consent	3	13
Theft of Bicycle	0	12
Theft of Vehicle	5	2
Theft Over $200.00	1	2
Theft Under $200.00	6	31
Unlawfully in a Dwelling	0	2
Wilful Damage	0	15
Total Charges Laid & Deferred Actions .	106	380

(Youth Branch continued
on the next page)

Increases:

Crime Statistics	increased by	684 cases	or 9.62% over 1979.
Theft Under $200.00	increased by	20 cases	or 0.84% over 1979.
Theft Over $200.00	increased by	81 cases	or 15.08% over 1979.
Traffic Fatalities	increased by	2 cases	or 66.67% over 1979.
Damage to Property	increased by	$155,159.00	or 62.54% over 1979.
Causing a Disturbance	increased by	28 cases	or 127.27% over 1979.
Break, Enter & Theft	increased by	209 cases	or 24.16% over 1979.
Robberies	increased by	4 cases	or 8.33% over 1979.
Fraud	increased by	12 cases	or 3.49% over 1979.
Auto Thefts	increased by	56 cases	or 31.46% over 1979.
Shoplifting Charges:			
Adult - Male	increased by	51 cases	or 67.11% over 1979.

Decreases:

Traffic Collisions	decreased by	242 cases	or 11.41% over 1979.
Injuries in Collisions	decreased by	69 cases	or 21.90% over 1979.
Assault Common	decreased by	14 cases	or 9.86% over 1979.
Vandalism	decreased by	186 cases	or 18.81% over 1979.
Skipping Bail	decreased by	31 cases	or 29.25% over 1979.
Shoplifting Charges:			
Adult - Female	decreased by	28 cases	or 19.44% over 1979.
Juvenile - Female	decreased by	4 cases	or 50.00% over 1979.
Assault Bodily Harm	decreased by	8 cases	or 32.00% over 1979.

Prosecution Summary:

Criminal Code Prosecutions decreased by 225 cases or 16.38% over 1979.

Deferred Actions C.C.C. Juveniles decreased by 21 cases or 5.22% over 1979.

Conclusions in solving criminal cases resulted in a 44.94% clearance rate or a decrease or 2.11% over 1979.

Traffic Charges including Parking Violations increased by 2,213 cases or 12.26% over 1979.

Modern communications and the influence of its instruments and techniques quickly spread patterns of criminality from one community to another, the City of Nepean is no exception.

The fact is that all citizens have at least the potential for illegal behaviour and therefore it is evident that crime is endemic in society as a whole and that our expectation of the criminal justice system should not be that it will eradicate crime but only that it will control it within "acceptable" limits.

I am proud of the record of this Force for the past year, a record accomplished by the concerted efforts of the members of this Force and the support and guidance of the Board of Commissioners of Police.

E.O. Wersch,
Chief of Police.

The 1980 Nepean City Police excerpts from the annual report shows the workload in the various categories and the success rate.

During 1981 the activities covered basically the same number of situations investigated by the Nepean City Police.

1957-1982...25 Years Service Celebrated with the Gloucester Township Police

1982 was the Nepean Police Forces 25th re-union, commencing in 1957 with the joint Gloucester-Nepean Police until 1964 and then continued as the Nepean Township Police until 1978, which changed the Township designation to city status, then continued as The City of Nepean Police Service until 1994.

History of the Nepean Police service is continued.

CRIME PREVENTION HANDBOOK, published by the Nepean Police and distributed to 27,000 homes and businesses in Nepean, with an additional 10,000 copies reserved at the Nepean City Police headquarters to be handed out to new residents and visitors in a campaign to reduce crime.

This was a well received book containing 48 pages of home and business security information.

(Photo from files in 2007)

The Nepean Crime prevention Unit traveled throughout the community holding information sessions at Schools, Shopping Malls and at Special community days, Constable Steve Marshall headed the program.

Nepean City Police Crime Prevention Field Unit working with the residents of the community.

25 Years Service Cake Cutting

Deputy Chief Wm. Brown Gloucester, Reeve D.A. Moodie, Nepean, Chief Gus Wersch Tim Halderson Nepean Police Association and Gloucester Association Representative.

POLICE BUILDINGS
1957 – 1982

Billings Bridge

Leitrim

Merivale Road

Bells Corners

Greenbank Road

**We
care . . .**

**. . . we
listen**

**Help
us
to help
you!**

POLICE VEHICLES
1967 – 1982

1967

1975

1968

1980

1969

1981

1973

1982

1974

1982

Nepean Police charity Blues getting ready to play a charity Hockey Game at the Ottawa Civic Centre in support of the Ken Spratt Memorial Charity.

Ken Spratt Memorial – Charity Police Hockey

The Nepean City Police Association were involved in many charity programs, to raise funds for special needs in the community, such as the Annual Area Police Hockey Tournament as shown in photo above.

The Nepean Police Charity Blues Foundation, was the first Registered Police Charity in Canada.

The Nepean Police Association raised funds for the Queensway Carleton Hospital. Sufficient funds were raised to purchase a trauma stretcher for the emergency room, and raised funds through a variety of programs to support charitable groups.

The Nepean Police Charity Blues Foundation raised over $300,000 dollars in funds to support:

- The Queensway Carleton Hospital palliative care
- Big Brothers
- Bereaved Families
- Hearing Loss Association
- The M.A.D.D. program

The Nepean Police Charity Blues Foundation was established in 1986. The founding members of the Nepean Police Association were: Officers of the Force – Devon Fermoyle, Tim Halderson, Harold Adams and Dave Ashton.

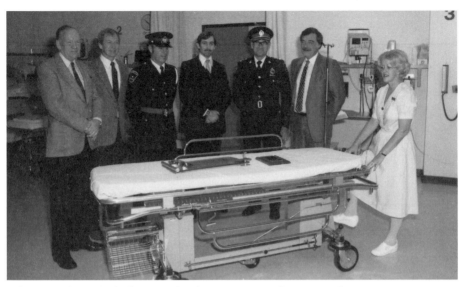

Fully equipped stretcher bed presented to the Queensway Carleton Hospital trauma emergency room.

Another program such as the Operation Go Home was supported by the Nepean Police to locate and bring back home wayward youths who left home and reunite them with their families.

Rev. Norm Johnson, Police Chaplain, headed the Operation Go Home program. Seen in photo at a sign with Rev. Johnson, Chief Gus Wersch and Cst. Sue Postlethwaite

Special programs were initiated by the School Safety Officer and to enhance the training of safe cycling. Awards were given to school patrollers at a Bicycle Jamboree. Fifteen bicycles and plaques were awarded to the winners supported by the management of the Bayshore Shopping Centre.

Shown with the winners, Back Row L.to R. Chief Wersch, Cst. Steve Marshall, Lou Boulanger General Manager and his Assistant of Bayshore Shopping centre.

Constable Steve Gilders helping a youngster playing with tricycle on the street.

The school patrollers were rewarded by a special visit to Government House to meet her Excellency Lily Schreyer, wife of the Governor General of Canada.

The following photograph shows Her Excellency pinning a school patroller's badge on one of the many patrollers that attended.

This was a first for the young students who served on the front line of the school crosswalks in the City of Nepean.

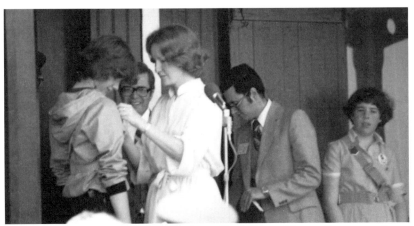

Her Excellency Lily Schreyer pinning school patrol badge on recipient at Government House.

A typical school crossing in a residential neighborhood, with Cst. John Wilkinson giving a safety lecture and hands on instruction to the School Patrollers.

Remembrance Day Annual Participation by the Nepean Police

A Remembrance Day Ceremony was held at the front of the Nepean Township Hall each year with representation from various organizations from Nepean involved in the wreath laying and moment of silence. The Nepean Police had a contingent of officers on parade at the November 11th annual service.

Chief Ewart Gus Wersch, representing the Nepean Police, giving the salute after laying wreath in remembrance of fallen soldiers at the front of the Nepean Township Hall at 3825 Richmond Road, Bells Corners.

Nepean Township Police on parade at the annual Remembrance Day service

The Annual Memorial Service for police and correctional officers killed in the line of duty is held at Parliament Hill, Ottawa. The service is held on a Sunday in September of each year.

A Book of Honour is displayed within the main foyer of the Parliament Buildings. This special event was authorized in 1977. See collage of photos on following page.

Nepean Police Officers attending Fallen Officers Service at Parliament Hill Ottawa.

A Canadian Police Service

Police Killed on Duty Remembrance Day photos on Parliament Hill, Ottawa

1983 and 1984 Nepean City Police Officers Killed And Injured On Duty

1983 and 1984 could be considered as the Nepean City Police's most difficult times. We were always concerned about the safety of Officers on patrol and while attending to domestic disputes, as these were sometimes the most volatile confrontations.

The officers were prepared to meet these challenges, but were not expecting to get that dreadful call from the Bayshore Shopping Centre on October 14th, 1983 – "Nepean Police Patrol Officer was shot and the situation was serious."

This concern became a reality when Constable David Utman was on patrol at the Bayshore Shopping Centre on October 14th, 1983. He had just sat down to discuss a few things at a coffee bar with staff at the centre, when a young male came to where he was sitting with a firearm in his hand. Constable Utman stood up and tried to talk the individual into giving up the firearm while slowly moving away from other civilians in the area.

Constable Utman never drew his gun but was shot in his chest by the male person leaving him to die on shopping centre floor. Constable Utman was killed for no apparent reason, and when the suspect was arrested a short time later he openly stated that he didn't like the police. He was out on parole at the time.

Constable Utman just happened to be a convenient target. The officer left a wife and two small children. It was one the most difficult times in my life at the formal funeral when I had to present the widow with the officer's uniform cap and flag from the coffin as part of the farewell ceremony.

A medal of bravery was issued and given to the wife posthumously at a special awards ceremony in Toronto by the Lt. Governor for the Province of Ontario in 1984.

Constable David Utman joined the Nepean Township Police May 1st, 1973 and had been assigned to General Patrol duties at the time he was killed on October 14th, 1983.

It was a senseless Criminal act which was totally unforeseen. He served with courage and bravery when confronted in a busy area of the shopping centre. By his actions he no doubt saved other peoples' lives, by attempting to talk the criminal into putting his gun down, while walking towards the center of mall area away from other shoppers, so that in the event of any shooting it would be out of immediate harm's way to others in the area.

We will remember him. A Nepean park has been named in his memory on Longfields Drive in Nepean.

Constable David UTMAN
We cherish his memory… May his light shine on forever.

Barrhaven Independent, Saturday, October 23, 1999

Park named in memory of fallen police officer

By Michelle Rickard
Independent Staff

Walking behind a 1964 Chevrolet Belair police cruiser with the badge number 53 on it, dozens of police officers and members of the Longfields-Davidson Heights community participated in the park dedication of a Nepean police officer who was killed in the line of duty 16 years ago.

Utman Park, located across from Mother Teresa High School on Longfields Drive, was officially named after David Utman who was killed during a robbery at the Bayshore Shopping Centre Oct. 14, 1983.

During a ceremony last Saturday morning, Mr. Utman was praised for his courage and sacrifice.

"I do hope our presence here to day will serve as a reminder to the Utman family and community that we haven't forgotten David's courage and sacrifice," said Nepean-Carleton MP David Pratt, adding, "We should never allow ourselves to forget people in the community."

Gus Wersch, a retired Nepean Township Chief of Police, said Mr. Utman was a person who served beyond the call of duty to protect his community.

"He was killed for no reason, a senseless act. It also killed part of our community as he was an extension of all of us, an extension of your peace and safety," he said. "Let us not forget him but remember him with this park dedication."

In a moment of silence, Pat Hayes, a district inspector with the Ottawa-Carleton Regional Police, played a portion of Amazing Grace on the bag pipes.

Nepean Councillor Wayne Phillips said Mr. Utman would have gotten a kick out of the fact that a park was being named after him.

THE ONTARIO MEDAL
FOR POLICE BRAVERY
AWARDED POSTHUMOUSLY TO
CONSTABLE DAVID UTMAN
NEPEAN POLICE FORCE
NOVEMBER 1, 1984

On October 14th, 1983 Constable David Utman was killed on duty by a gunman for no apparent reason. The incident occurred at a busy Shopping Centre. Cst. Utman attempted to talk the gunman into surrending, at the same time moving away from the public.

The Medal and Citation was awarded to Constable Utman's two children at a Ceremony in Toronto on November 1st, 1984. Constable Utman will always be remembered for his extreme act of Bravery and Courage.

E.G. Wersch,
Chief of Police.

**Chief E. Gus Wersch, Premier Bill Davis, Lt. Gov. Gen Ontario J. Aird
Mrs. Utman and Children Bravery Awards presentations 1984
In Memory of David Utman killed on Duty Oct 14th, 1983**

One Year later in September 1984 – ANOTHER Nepean Police tragedy at the Same Bayshore Shopping Centre

Serious injuries to Constable Robin Easey and Constable Ralph Erfle. (Crime Scene next Pages)

Actual scene of shooting by armed robbers and Nepean Police Officers, where Cst. Robin Easey and Cst. Ralph Erfle were wounded September 1984.

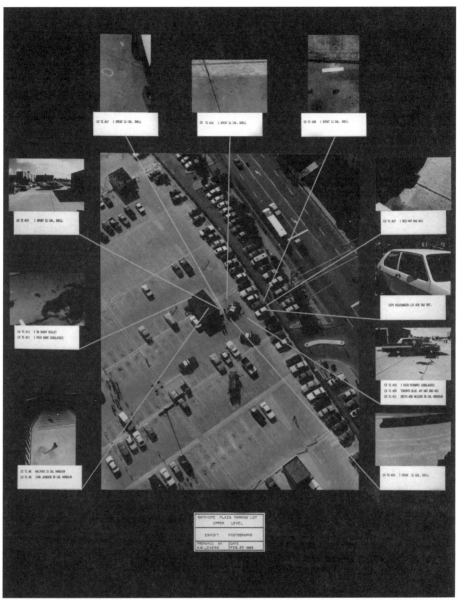

For court presentation, crime scene of: Attempted robbery of armored vehicle bringing funds to the Bayshore Shopping Centre.September 1984.

Constable Erfle and Constable Easey were called to the Bayshore Shopping Centre to check out a suspicious person.

When the officers arrived a gun battle ensued. Apparently five persons had planned to take down an armoured vehicle carrying funds to the centre which was late. This made the suspects edgy, so when the police arrived they were in position to surprise Constable Easy while he was questioning one of the suspects, the other shot him in the neck at close range.

It was at this time that Constable Erfle arrived and was confronted with a barrage of fire from the suspects. He shot one suspect in the forehead instantly killing him but ran out of ammo. As he was in the patrol car calling for back up and reloading, another suspect approached and fired at close range striking him in his jaw and thigh, shattering his thigh bone. The suspect then aimed at his head but the gun had jammed, so the remaining suspects jumped into a car and fled leaving the two officers in a serious injured state.

Constable Easey survived but is permanently disabled. His loss of blood and head injury left him blind and he has difficulty walking without assistance. He is on a life long disability. Although he can talk, he is left with only a short term memory.

I find it amazing that he has come as far as he has, and one thing that is unexplainable is that his short term memory relates to things he does from day to day, but his long term memory relates to voices of persons he has worked with in the past.

I have approached him after not seeing him for a few months or more, and say how are you doing Robin, (his first name), he responds by moving his head in my direction and without hesitation says, "It's the Chief" with a smile on his face.

Although he is well looked after, his family of two small children and his wife had to suffer through this ordeal.

This incident once again shows how vulnerable a police officer on the beat is – from when an innocent call of a suspicious person erupts into one robber dead and two police officers seriously injured

Officers wounded at Bayshore Shopping Centre 1984:

Constable Robin Easey

Constable Ralph Erfle

Constable Ralph Erfle recovered and returned to duty within the year after the incident and is still a member of the Police Force. Both officers received a Medal for Bravery presented to them in a special ceremony by the Lt. Governor for the Province of Ontario, plus many other citations.

A special letter of recognition and encouragement was received from the President of the United States over the signature of President Ronald Reagan, addressed to Cst. Robin Easey.

Constable Robin Easey spent many months in the head injury unit of the hospital at Cortland in New York State.

Constable Easey remains a member of the Nepean Police, and is supported under the Workers Compensation Plan as well as staying on salary until his official retirement date. He is supported by a home based attendant and lives at home with his family.

On September 1st, 1984, Constable Robin Easey and Constable Ralph Erfle responded to a suspicious persons call at the Bayshore Shopping Centre. Upon their arrival, it became obvious that a group of criminals were in the process of robbing an armoured vehicle bringing funds to the Centre. In the confrontation, both officers were seriously wounded and one of the suspects was killed. Their courage and bravery were recognized by the Province of Ontario on December 9th, 1985 when Lieutenant Governor Lincoln Alexander presented both officers with the Highest Medal for Bravery at the Parliament Buildings in Toronto.

E.G. Wersch,
Chief of Police.

Constable Robin Easey and Constable Ralph Erfle receiving Bravery Rewards from Lt. Governor General Lincoln Alexander, of Ontario, at a Special Awards night held in 1985 at Toronto

A few years later.

While attending the opening of the new City of Nepean Hall at 101 Centrepointe Drive, in April 1988, Cst.Robin Easey also visited the Nepean Police Headquarters with the following: Glennis Easey, Sherry Franklin, Lt. Gov. Lincoln Alexander and Mrs. Alexander, Mayor Ben Franklin, Cst.. Robin Easey and Chief Ewart Gus Wersch.

THE WHITE HOUSE

WASHINGTON

November 4, 1985

Dear Robin:

I have been meaning to write you since your situation was brought to my attention by Richard Troyer of the Cortland Police Department. As you know, all of the Cortland officers are Robin boosters and I'm proud to join them.

Private citizens tend to forget that the men and women who wear the badge take serious, sometimes fatal, risks every day they are on patrol. Police officers never forget it, however, and certainly I will never forget it, since a Washington, D.C., police officer was seriously injured when he stopped a bullet that was aimed at me four years ago. So, in a way you symbolize the bravest men and women in a profession in which bravery is a commonplace.

I am told you are making progress in your therapy, Robin, and I know you have the courage and strength of purpose to fight this thing through. You are very lucky to have a wife who is pulling for you all the way. Good luck and God bless you both.

Sincerely,

Ronald Reagan

Constable Robin Easey
Highgate Manor Nursing Home
28 Kellogg Road
Cortland, New York 13045

The 1983 Plowing Match

The 1983 Plowing Match was held in the City of Nepean between Richmond Road and Eagleson Side Road in September 1983. The following photos show the early use of oxen, horses and steam powered equipment for use on farms.

Team of oxen, used in early development of agricultural land.
1983 City of Nepean Hosts International Plowing Match.

Demonstration of plowing the old fashioned way

Chief out looking for new equipment!

Chief out recruiting

The Chief can pitch it with the best!

Old Steam engine "Titan"

Team of six horses proudly showing off their ability

Opening of Nepean's new city hall, 1988

Nepean Police Officers on the ready to assist at the Official Opening of new Nepean City Hall on April 29th, 1988

Time Capsule: Photographs of vault in the new City of Nepean Hall located in main entrance floor. March 18th, 1988

Lowering time capsule into floor vault located in main entrance floor of Nepean City Hall located on Centrepointe Drive.

Vault to be opened 100 years hence, March 18th, 2088.

Chief Gus Wersch, Mayor Ben Franklin, and Al Brown, Merv Beckstead Commissioner of Finance lower the capsule into the vault. The vault contains City of Nepean artifacts from the City Departments, Nepean Police Letter, Badges, etc. and is scheduled to be opened in 2088 (100 Years).

Mayor Ben Franklin and Member of Council Al Brown sealing vault in floor.

Officers at Nepean Police Centre 245 Greenbank Road.

Cutting Ribbon at Official Opening of new Nepean City Hall at Centrepointe Drive, April 29th, 1988. Officiating Lt. Gov General Lincoln Alexander and Mayor Ben Franklin.

Opening of Nepean City Hall, April 1988, attended by Lt. Governor Lincoln ALexander and Mayor Ben Franklin.

NEPEAN POLICE FORCE

245 GREENBANK ROAD, NEPEAN, ONTARIO, K2H 8W9
PHONE 829-2211

ADDRESS ALL CORRESPONDENCE TO CHIEF OF POLICE

MEMBER

E. G. WERSCH
Chief of Police

March 1, 1988

Your ref. No. _____

Our ref. No. _____

To Whom It May Concern:

Re: Nepean Police Force - 1988

Dear Citizens of Nepean:

It is a pleasure to have had the opportunity to participate in the development of police services in the City of Nepean for the past 39 years. My philosophy has always been to accept change not for the sake of change, but for a positive move ahead. The concerns in 1988 are in many instances continuous from the past and will not be resolved in the immediate future. It would be "Utopia" if we could realize a crime-free society.

The age-old problem of alcohol and increases in the use of drugs today has become a very serious issue. The effort to reduce impaired driving when having consumed alcohol and/or drugs is a daily task. Home security is a present day issue; residents are involved in programs to prevent residential and business break, enter and thefts. Child abuse, concern for victims of crime and disrespect for personal and public property continues to be an issue.

The foregoing may indicate that we in Nepean have a serious crime problem. This is not the case as the crime rate is relatively low on a per capita basis as compared to other areas of the country. We have a dynamic community and the Nepean Police Force has maintained it's mandate to keep the peace and provide for a safe place in which to live.

For the past ten years we have computerized and automated our records and communication systems and are continuing to stay at the leading edge of high technology.

In conclusion, I wish you well and hope you enjoy the fruits of our labours as we have left our footprints in the sands of time.

Yours sincerely,

E. G. Wersch,
Chief of Police.

EGW/ra

NOTE: ORIGINAL COPY OF THIS LETTER PLACED IN SEALED COMPARTMENT WITH OTHER HISTORIC ITEMS IN FLOOR OF ATRIUM AT NEPEAN CITY HALL 101 CENTREPOINTE TO BE OPENED IN "2088"(100 YRS).

RIDEAU HALL
OTTAWA

On the occasion of	À l'occasion du
the twenty-fifth Anniversary	vingt-cinquième anniversaire
of the accession of	de l'accession de
HER MAJESTY THE QUEEN	SA MAJESTÉ LA REINE
to the Throne	au Trône
the accompanying medal	la médaille ci-jointe
is presented to	est remise à

Ewart Gustav Wersch

1952 ~ 1977

Certificate: The Queen's Jubilee Medal is awarded to police officers who served 25 years during 1952-1977 by The Governor General of Canada of the day. In my case it was His Excellency Governor General Jules Leger.

As the Nepean Police Officers reached their 20 years of service, they are awarded with a medal and every five years thereafter with a bar and one star, which has another star added after the next five years.

They are awarded the above mentioned service medals as well as the Queen's Jubilee Medal.

Police Exemplary Service Medal
Médaille de la Police pour Services Distingués

a
Replica of the Medal
awarded to

une
Reproduction de la Médaille
décernée à

on behalf of
The Governor General of Canada

au nom de
Le Gouverneur Général du Canada

1952-1977 in recognition for service to Canada and Nepean in particular.

THE SECOND AWARD OF
THE POLICE EXEMPLARY
SERVICE MEDAL

has been granted to

E.G. WERSCH

in recognition of thirty years of loyal and meritorious service to law enforcement in Canada.

Governor General of Canada

Police Service and Queen's Jubilee Medals

CHAPTER 7: NEPEAN POLICE FORCE

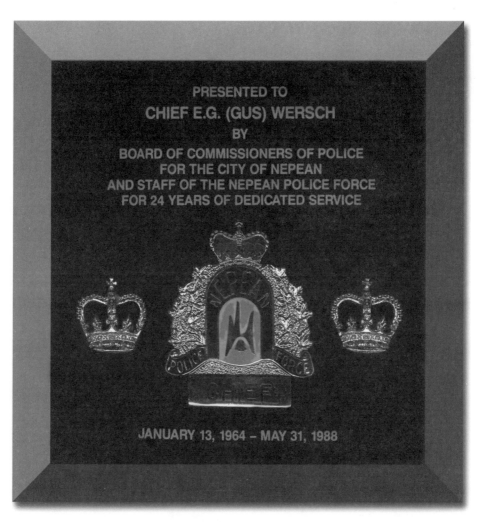

Cap Badge and Collar Dogs worn by Chief E. Gus Wersch and presented to him on retirement May 31st, 1988.

In recognition of 24 years service to the Nepean Police Service, by the Board of Nepean Police Commissioners.

NEPEAN POLICE SERVICE MEDAL AWARDS

Sgt W. Story, Sgt B. Easey, Sgt N. Parks, Sgt C. Raganold, Sgt P. Monette

Insp. R. Lamont, S/Insp W. Chaykowski, Chief E. Gus Wersch
Insp. B. Henry   and Insp R. Elstone

CHIEF WERSCH'S 1988 POLICE FAMILY

The following pages relate to a Special Recognition Program for the Nepean Police Service to the Community 1964-1994, headed by Margaret Rywak, Nepean Councillor. Her dedication to the police community and her untiring effort to put this program together was greatly appreciated.

One Moment in Time

A Commemorative Ceremony
to Honour
Nepean Police Officers
1964-1994

Nepean Civic Square, 101 Centrepointe Drive

September 14, 1997
2 p.m.

Program Participants

Mayor Ben Franklin
City of Nepean

Councillor Margaret Rywak
Councillor, Knoxdale Ward
Chair, Nepean Police Service
Commemorative Committee

Chief Gus Wersch
Chief of Nepean Police Service
1966 - 1988

Chief Wayne Phillips
Chief of Nepean Police Service
1988 - 1994

The Reverend Robert Heard
Rector, St. Martin's Anglican Church
Chaplain, Ottawa-Carleton Regional Police Service
Honorary Staff/Inspector

Soloist, Trish Grierson
Staff Member, Human Resources,
Ottawa-Carleton Regional Police Service
(Formerly a staff member of the Nepean Police Service)

Accompanist, Bill Wilson
Co-director of Regional Police Service Choir

Piper, John MacMillan
Member of Ottawa-Carleton Regional Police Pipe Band

Councillor Margaret Rywak shaking hands with Chief Gus Wersch – Mayor Ben Franklin

Special plaque with all the names of Police Officers who served in Nepean 1964–1994 installed at the Nepean City Hall in the main foyer.

Plaque with names engraved of officers who served in the Nepean Police Service, 1964–1994.

(List of names of officers on next two pages from Moment in Time programme includes names of Officers on active service, resignations, and those who passed away from natural causes during 1964-1994.)

Nepean Police 1964- 1994

Chief John Rankin
(January 1, 1964 to March 31, 1966)

Chief Ewart Gus Wersch
(April 1, 1966 to May 31, 1988)

Chief Wayne Phillips
(June 1, 1988 to December 31, 1994)

Cst. Harold Adams
Sgt. David Andrew
Sgt. Timothy Armour
Sgt. Stewart Arnott
Cst. David Ashton
Cst. Mark Barclay
Sgt. Gerry Barker
Cst. Clifford Bastien
Cst. Rohan Beebakhee
Sgt. Robert Behan
Cst. Steven Berry
Cst. Kevin Birmingham
Cst. Lachlan Bisaillion
Cst. Stephen Blackburn
Cst. Leanne Blais
Cst. Laurie Boon
Cst. Mark Bornais
Cst. Paul Bosley
Sgt. Frederick Bowie
Cst. Shaun Brabazon
S/Sgt. Garry Briese
Cst. Bradley Brown
Cst. Norman Bruce
Sgt. Paul Bullied
Cst. Tracy Butler
Sgt. James Cameron
Cst. Rene Cardinal
Cst. Gary Cashman
Cst. Jacques Champagne

Sgt. Richard Chapman
S/Sgt. Thomas Chapman
Sgt. Paul Charlebois
S/Insp. Walter Chaykowski
S/Sgt. Terry Cheslock
Cst. Monica Christian
Sgt. Thomas Collins
Cst. Richard Comba
Cst. David Conroy
Cst. William Costello
Cst. Donegal Coulson
Sgt. Maurice Coyle
S/Insp. Peter Cuthbert
Sgt. William Dalton
Cst. Paul Davey
Insp. Gordon Deavy
Cst. Robert de Hartog
Sgt. Paul Delahay
Cst. Norman Deneault
Cst. Ronald Desormeaux
Cst. James Devine
Cst. Wayne Dixon
Cst. Thomas Donnelly
S/Sgt. Ronald Driscoll
Cst. Anthony Duncan
Cst. Paul Dunlop
S/Sgt. Herbert Easey
Sgt. Robin Easey
Cst. John Elliott
Insp. Ronald Elstone
S/Sgt. Ralph Erfle
Sgt. John Ethier
D/Chief Devon Fermoyle
Insp. Ian Fiegenwald
Cst. James Fitzgibbons
Sgt. Patrick Flanagan
S/Sgt. David Forbes

Cst. Leslie Frost
Cst. Robert Gagne
S/Sgt. Frederick Gardner
Cst. Mark Gatien
Cst. Ronald Gervais
Cst. Kalid Ghadban
Cst. Stephen Gilders
Cst. Kenneth Giroux
Cst. Calvin Goble
Cst. Harold Godwin
Cst. James Goodyer
Insp. Murray Gordon
Cst. Stephen Gorgichuk
Cst. Donald Graves
Cst. Richard Guay
Sgt. Timothy Halderson
Cst. Andrew Hamilton
Cst. Geoffrey Hamlin
Cst. Bruce Harwood
Cst. Robert Havens
Insp. Bud Henry
Cst. Jay Hitchins
Cst. Paul Holland
Cst. Wayne Holland
Cst. Peter Howe
Cst. Chris Hrnchiar
Cst. Lee Jones
Cst. Richard Jones
Cst. Sherry Jordan
Cst. Jamie Jordon
Cst. Edward Kaminski
Cst. Blake Keays
Cst. Stephen Kellett
Cst. Theresa Kelm
Cst. Douglas Kightley
Cst. James Killeen
Cst. Bruce King

Dedicated to Those Who Served

Cst. Julia Kinkade
Cst. John Kiss
Cst. Gilbert Knox
Cst. Shawn Ku
Cst. Donna Kuechle
Cst. David Lacharity
Cst. Raymond Lamarre
D/Chief Ronald Lamont
Cst. Sharon Lamont
Cst. Christopher Lamourie
Cst. Jeffrey Langevin
Cst. Marc Lecelles
Cst. Timothy Legate
Sgt. Wayne Levere
Cst. Arthur Lewis
Cst. Kenneth Livingstone
Cst. Kenneth Logan
Cst. Daniel Longpre
Cst. Barrie MacDonald
Sgt. Murdock Macleod
Cst. Donna MacNeil-Charbot
Cst. William MacWilliam
S/Sgt. Robert Mancuso
Cst. Michael Marelic
Cst. Rodney Marks
Cst. Bruce Marshall
Cst. Stephen Marshall
Cst. Peter Martin
Cst. Wayne Mattingly
Cst. Allan McConnell
Cst. Michael McCormack
Sgt. Lawrence McCourt
Cst. Sean McDade
Cst. John McDonald
Cst. Shawn McDonald
Insp. Brian McGarvey
Cst. Christopher McGuinness

Cst. James McGuire
Sgt. John McKay
Cst. Larry McNally
S/Sgt. Gary Meehan
Cst. Blaine Mercier
Cst. Terry Milton
Cst. John Monette
S/Sgt. Peter Monette
Cst. Alex Moraru
Cst. Keith Morrell
Cst. Lawrence Moyer
Cst. William Murrell
Cst. Mark Myers
Cst. Christopher Niblett
S/Sgt. Geoffrey Nichol
Cst. Trevor O'Donovan
Cst. Linda Ogilvie
Cst. Christopher Parent
Insp. Nyall Parks
Cst. Christopher Partridge
Cst. Jeffrey Patterson
Sgt. Anda Pember
Cst. Robert Pember
Cst. Keith Pittam
Cst. Susan Postlethwaite
S/Sgt. Clifford Raganold
Cst. Maria Ragudo
Cst. Jacques Richard
Cst. Peter Richard
Insp. Knowlton Roberts
Sgt. Melvin Robertson
Cst. Phillip Robinson
Cst. Joanne Rooke
Sgt. Raymond Sabourin
Cst. Edward St. Denis
Cst. Raymond St. Pierre
Cst. Ross Saunders

Cst. Leslie Scott
Cst. Brian Sharpe
Sr./Sgt. James Sheahan
Cst. Daniel Simser
Sgt. Haddon Smith
Sgt. Alferio Spadaccini
Cst. Paul Spirak
Sgt. Bradley Spriggs
Cst. Shaun Steele
S/Sgt. Wayne Stephenson
Cst. David Stewart
Sgt. Willard Story
Sgt. Clifford Sullivan
Cst. William Taylor
Cst. Richard Tennant
Cst. Tapinder Thind
Cst. David Thomas
Cst. Bradford Tierney
S/Sgt. Gerry Trudel
Cst. Michael Ueltzhoffer
Cst. Daryl Upshaw
Cst. David Utman*
Cst. Jake Vanderlei
Cst. William Van Ryswyk
Cst. Charles Walters
Sgt. Douglas Warren
Cst. Kenneth Whitehorne
Sgt. John Wilkinson
Cst. Kenneth Williams
Cst. Douglas Wilson
Cst. Paul Wilson
Cst. Leigh Wood
D/Chief Richard Zanibbi

Killed in the line of duty

Program

The Chambers

Invocation Prayer .... The Reverend Robert Heard

O Canada .... Soloist, Trish Grierson

Welcome & Introduction of Council Members .... Mayor Ben Franklin

Opening Remarks &
Acknowledgment of Special Guests .... Councillor Margaret Rywak,

Remarks .... Mayor Ben Franklin

History of Service
1964 - 1988 .... Chief Ewart Gus Wersch

History of Service .... Chief Wayne Phillips
1988 - 1994

Solo - "One Moment in Time" .... Trish Grierson

The Atrium

Dedication Prayer .... The Reverend Robert Heard

Plaque Unveiling .... Chief Wersch & Chief Phillips

"One Moment in Time" .... Trish Grierson

Closing Remarks .... Councillor Rywak

God Save the Queen

Reception

Hosted by Nepean City Council:

Mayor Ben Franklin, Councillor Doug Collins, Councillor Lee Farnworth,
Councillor Margaret Rywak, Councillor Molly McGoldrick-Larsen,
Councillor Rick Chiarelli and Councillor Merv Sullivan.

09-28-97

Dear Gus,

Well, we certainly pleased a lot of people on the 14th. How can I thank you for coming on the Committee and giving so much to make the day a huge success? Frankly, I don't know what we would have done without you. It just would have been a less elaborate affair. The memorabilia was just wonderful. From the pictures you can see how people enjoyed it. Everything you contributed, even the leaves, added so much.

It was overdue and I think it has left a good feeling about the City with the officers. I am not sure that was the case before. Thanks again, Gus, for everything. Sincerely, Margaret

Letter from Councillor Margaret Rywak

Photos of display boards depicting Nepean Police Activity 1964-1994

Photo of Nepean Police 1957-1982

Police Badges & Insignias.

General Action Photos

Constable Wayne Levere treating resident to donut at Tim Hortons.

Thor: our search and rescue dog.
Cst. Mark Gatien was Thor's handler.

Police Buildings 1964–1994

Photo at the Nepean Police Museum Display: Chief Wersch trying to type his memoirs on an antique typewriter.

Chief Wersch talking to a manniquin at the Nepean Museum Police Display Nov. 2nd, 2008.

Chief Wersch standing beside Nepean Police "Car 53". Car 53 is still used for promotional events and is held in the custody of the Regional Police since amalgamation in 1994. Photo taken when on display at the Nepean Museum.

Cell Block

*Cell Block Keys from Nepean Police Bells Corners Station
1966–1978, Historical Items*

NEPEAN
a mark of progress

On November 29, 1978 the new Nepean Police Head-quarters was officially opened. Centrally located in a large sprawling urban area adjacent to the city of Ottawa, the building combines a functional plan with an esthetically pleasing appearance. Facing on Greenbank Road, one of the municipality's north-south arteries, the site is landscaped, providing a parkland setting for the structure, with staff parking and operational access at the rear of the building, well shielded from public view. The two storey basic structure is reinforced concrete flat slab, supported on reinforced concrete columns with piled foundations. The exterior cladding is precast concrete and brick, and the structure is designed to allow for construction of three more floors for future expansion.

The opening was attended by municipal, provincial and federal representatives, members of Nepean Council and Board of Police Commissioners, and guests who were treated to a tour of the modern police structure and its many new facilities. Nepean Mayor, Andrew Haydon*, Sidney Handleman, the provincial member who represented Premier William Davis of Ontario, Walter Baker, member of parliament for Grenville-Carleton, and Chief Wersch, Nepean police, officiated. Mayor Haydon and Mr. Handleman unveiled a large granite plaque that will serve as a memorial to the occasion. An Ontario and a Canadian flag were donated respectively by Mr. Handleman and Mr. Baker, and handed over to Chief Wersch. The flags are flown from the masts in front of the police building.

The building boasts some of the most modern facilities, from solar heating (which may be a first for a police building in Canada) to a sauna bath for the troops. The structure is equipped with an emergency electrical generator for 24 hour power supply; closed circuit TV for security entrances and cells; electrically operated security door locks; and a new communications system with console and an around-the-clock complaint and radio communications logger.

The mechanical systems which embrace the heating and cooling facilities (both incorporating solar assist) were designed to complement the architectural concept. The square shape of the floor plan with its high ratio interior and perimeter spaces, added thermal insulation, and reflecting glass throughout will contribute to lower peak heating and cooling loads. A unique feature of the solar system (in addition to its auxiliary heat) is its provision of year-round domestic hot water for equipment wash bays, showers for the cells, and service hot water.

The main floor (upper level) has a gross area of 19,150 square feet. The public entrance faces west and is accessible from Greenbank Road. Immediately accessible from the lobby is the information desk and records retrieval areas.

The Records Section and adjoining Communications Branch form the central core from which numerous offices radiate. The specially designed console in the Communications Branch contains built-in radio and telephone communications systems, controls for the closed circuit TV, security door controls and an illuminated status map. The security areas and entrances are monitored from this console using the closed circuit TV system. Surrounding this core are the various offices including the administration wing, boardroom, Youth Branch, Criminal Investigation Branch, Uniform Division, Traffic Branch and the School Safety Officer. The security area includes a drive-in bay, male and female holding cells, interview area, fingerprinting room, breathalyzer room, as well as witness and identification rooms, making it a secure and efficient prisoner receiving area. The drive-in bay which leads into the receiving and cell block area eliminates the moving of persons under arrest from vehicles in a parking lot and thus will eliminate completely any chance of escape.

The ground floor (lower level) has a gross area of 20,700 square feet. It comprises a combined training lecture room, and the entire area may be used for large scale meetings or as an emergency control centre. The exercise room adjacent to the meeting hall will be equipped to permit development of a physical culture program. This floor also contains a modern Identification Branch; locker and lunch rooms; stolen property/exhibit storage area; a workshop; a vehicle examination/identification garage; and a four-stall pistol range with firing points of fifteen, twenty and twenty-five yards.

The firearm range ventilation system is designed on a new energy saving concept whereby the smoke and toxic fumes are removed from the air through electric precipitators, filters and washdown. This uses only one quarter of the outdoor air for ventilation normally required with the traditional systems.

Operational access for police personnel is at the lower level from the parking lot at the east side of the building. Upon entrance, a footwear washup and coat dripping room is provided near the locker rooms. A muster (briefing) room for patrol staff, offices for supervisors, the training officer, and for report writing or dictating are also provided. Provision has also been made for a police library. Dictating facilities are completely automatic, with dictating booths located on both floors and the recording equipment situated in a steno pool in the central core area of the main floor.

A distinct impression gained from a tour of this building is that in its planning nothing has been overlooked. Although some research was undertaken in the matter of planning, certain design features have been incorporated not so much

*Since the official opening of the new Nepean Police Headquarters, Andrew Haydon, who for many years served as reeve in Nepean and chairman of the Board of Police Commissioners, has been appointed chairman of the Regional Municipality of Ottawa Carleton. The new mayor of Nepean is Ben Franklin, a former senior councillor.

from what had been observed in existing police buildings but rather from the imaginative thinking of the department collectively and from the obvious lack in existing designs of some of the amenities considered so desirable for staff morale as well as for practical operational needs.

The city of Nepean Police Force polices an area approximating 82 square miles with a population of about 80,000. The department comprises 101 regular members (including two policewomen) and 23 civilians. It is headed by Chief E.G. (Gus) Wersch, who is well known to CACP members through his active participation in the affairs of the Association over the past several years — first as a Sergeant-at-Arms, and currently as Secretary-Treasurer.

The policing of what is now Nepean municipality goes back to 1929 when a Carleton County police force was formed to serve the entire county, including the then township of Nepean. Nine years later the police force was disbanded and the area was patrolled by the Ontario Provincial Police. With rapid suburban development in the area during the war years, the first Nepean Township police department was formed on May 1, 1945. On January 1, 1950 however, Westboro, a suburb of Ottawa, was annexed by the city and a consequent reduction in the Nepean township population resulted in the elimination of the Nepean police. The Ontario Provincial Police then continued to serve the township as part of their responsibilities in Carleton County until July 1957.

As a municipal department the Nepean Force thus has had a rather unique history, beginning again on July 1, 1957 as a joint Gloucester-Nepean Township department headed by the late Chief John Rankin. With the rapid growth of Nepean and the geographical formation of the two townships (located almost at opposite extremes of the greater Ottawa area), a joint police force soon became impractical and the police department was split into two municipal forces. Thus, the Nepean police department as it is known today, was formed on January 1, 1964, with Chief Rankin in charge. Chief Rankin passed away in March 1966, and his second in command, then Sgt. E.G. Wersch, one of the original members of the Nepean department, was appointed Chief.

The opening of the new Nepean Police Headquarters was auspicious and worthy of historical note also for another reason — almost concurrently with the event (on November 24) the municipality of Nepean was officially declared a city by the province of Ontario, adding a new image and dimension to an area that has been more commonly known as a "suburb of Ottawa".

The city of Nepean is still a relatively sparse area, and if the last few years are any indication of its growth and aggressive community development, the future looks promising for it to become one of the most progressive little cities in the province. This prospect also augurs well for the police department which has enjoyed a reputation of good management, good policing and good community relations.

The city of Nepean and the Nepean Police Force are to be congratuated for their achievement, and we wish Chief Wersch and his department continued success.

We are pleased to reproduce a number of plans and photographs of the new Nepean police department and members wishing to obtain material or more information about it may write:

Chief E.G. Wersch,
Nepean Police Force,
245 Greenbank Road,
Nepean, Ontario.
K2H 8W9.

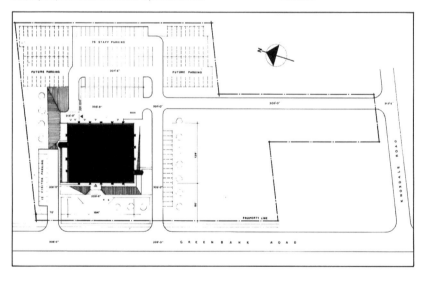

~ CHAPTER 8 ~

CONCLUSION

"Behind the Badge"

As I stated at the outset of this report, I joined the Ontario Provincial Police on November 1st, 1949, and after serving in that force until January 12th, 1964. I continued to Serve on the Nepean Police Force until May 31st, 1988. (The final 22 years as Chief of Police, retiring with over 38 years of service.)

The following items relate to my retirement from the Nepean Police Service effective May 31st, 1988.

Excerpts from my retirement celebrations where 540 people attended a farewell dinner function held on June 10th, 1988.

I received many plaques from police forces throughout Canada and the Province of Ontario in particular.

Letters were sent from The Prime Minister of Canada, Premier of Ontario, Judicial Branches, and many others along with a life membership from the Canadian Chiefs of Police Association, and the Ontario Chiefs of Police Association.

Many of these letters are included in the following pages.

PRIME MINISTER · PREMIER MINISTRE

Ottawa, K1A 0A2
May 18,1988

Dear Chief Wersch,

I am delighted to extend to you my sincere best wishes and congratulations on the occasion of your retirement as chief of the Nepean Police Force.

Over the years, you have had a long and distinguished career, one which you should reflect upon with pride in the days to come. Your efforts to ensure the safety and good order of the community are to be commended. As Prime Minister, may I express to you my sincere appreciation for your many years of commitment and dedication to the citizens of Nepean.

Mila and I would like to join with your family and many friends in wishing you the very best for a fulfilling and happy retirement.

With every good wish,

Yours sincerely,

Ontario

Office of the Minister	**Ministry of the Solicitor General**	25 Grosvenor Street Toronto, Ontario M7A 1Y6
Bureau du ministre	**Ministère du Solliciteur général**	25, rue Grosvenor Toronto (Ontario) M7A 1Y6

May 26, 1988

Telephone/Téléphone:
(416) 965-2021

Chief of Police E.G. Wersch
Nepean Police Force
245 Greenbank Road
NEPEAN, Ontario
K2H 8W9

Dear Chief Wersch:

May I join your many friends and colleagues in wishing you well on your retirement as Chief of Police for the City of Nepean.

For close to 40 years you have served the people of Nepean and Carleton County as a police officer. I am advised that you are one of the longest-serving police chiefs in Ontario, if not the country.

Through your work with the Canadian Association of Chiefs of Police, you have contributed to the advancement of policing across Canada.

All the best in the years ahead.

Sincerely,

Joan Smith

Joan Smith
Solicitor General

Canadian Association of Chiefs of Police

Association canadienne des Chefs de Police

Tower B, Place de Ville, Suite 1908
112 Kent St., Ottawa, Ontario, K1P 5P2
(613) 233-1106

Ref: SER-6-8

May 31, 1988

Mr. E.G. Wersch
68 Avonlea Road
Nepean, Ontario
K2G OJ5

Dear Mr. Wersch:

On behalf of the President and members of the Board of Directors, I welcome you to "Life" membership in the Canadian Association of Chiefs of Police.

The Association extends to you its best wishes for happiness in retirement. I hope that it will be possible for you to maintain contact with the many friends you have made among the members of the Association. I further hope that you will be able to attend the annual conference from time to time.

You will continue to receive the Canadian Police Chief newsletter.

Enclosed is your Life membership card and Certificate.

Yours sincerely,

D.N. Cassidy
Executive Director

DNC/jm

Encls.

The Premier
of Ontario

Le Premier ministre
de l'Ontario

Legislative Building
Queen's Park
Toronto, Ontario
M7A 1A1

Hôtel du gouvernement
Queen's Park
Toronto (Ontario)
M7A 1A1

June 10, 1988

Dear Mr. Wersch:

On the occasion of your retirement as
Chief of Police of the City of Nepean, I take
pleasure in extending warm congratulations and
sincere appreciation on behalf of the people and
the Government of Ontario.

Throughout a lifetime of work, you have
demonstrated a high level of personal integrity
and commitment. As Chief of Police you brought
these distinguished qualities to the service of
your fellow residents of Nepean.

As you are honoured this evening by
your many friends and colleagues, I join with
them in conveying gratitude for your contribution
to the quality of justice in your community, and
best wishes for happiness and fulfilment in your
retirement.

Sincerely,

David Peterson

```
                                        30 Lansfield Way
                                        Nepean, Ont.

                                        June 27th, 1988

Gus Wersch
68 Avonlea Rd.
Nepean, Ont.
K2G0J5

Dear Sir:

     I wish to congratulate you and to extend my best wishes for your retirement. I
also want to thank you for all you did for me, especially while I was recovering from
the Bayshore shooting. You were indeed very kind and considerate , both to me and my
parents.

     I am very impressed by your long and distinguished career which will always
serve as a form of motivation to me. I was also impressed by all the friends and
admirers you have made in this country, and in particular in Nepean. You have given
our police force one great reputation which hopefully will stand forever. The
procedures and policies you established within our department will continue for
years to come.

     Let me say once again that your leadership abilities and accomplishments will
always be remembered and be an inspiration to many career officers for years to come.

     Please take care of yourself and Fran and enjoy all life has to offer. Fran
is really a great woman who seems to know how to enjoy life to it's fullest. Remember
the metaphor Sgt. J. Cameron left us with, "Take time to smell the roses." I hope that
know you will be able to do this.

                                        Yours very truly,

                                        Ralph Erfle

P.S. I would still love to visit you at your cottage some time and take you up on
     the invitation.
```

Thanks to you, Ralph Erfle, for your sacrifice to the City of Nepean. We are forever indebted to you for a job well done and we all appreciated that you were able to continue in the Police Service.

Ewart Gus Wersch, Chief of Police, Nepean

THE LIEUTENANT GOVERNOR
QUEEN'S PARK
TORONTO, ONTARIO
M7A 1A1

July 12, 1988

Dear Chief Wersch:

I would like to take this opportunity to thank you for sending me the beautiful photographs taken during my visit to the Nepean Police Headquarters on April 29, 1988. Your thoughtfulness is very much appreciated.

It also gives me great pleasure to extend greetings to you on the occasion of your retirement from the Force. Your contribution to the community during the past 39 years of service is recognized and deeply appreciated.

Warm best wishes to you and your family for good health and happiness in all your future endeavours.

Yours sincerely,

Lincoln M. Alexander
Lieutenant Governor

Chief E.G. Wersch
c/o Nepean Police Force
245 Greenbank Road
Nepean, Ontario
K2H 8W9

June 27, 1988

Dear Gus,

First of all, I would like to thank you for the letter you
sent me on the occasion of your retirement. I personally
think you did an excellent job as Chief. We could not have
asked for a better or a fairer man. I only hope that I can
do my job as well as you did yours.

Thank you, too, for the support you gave me and my family
when I was injured. Glennis and I appreciate your concern
and encouragement.

I would like to wish you the best of luck in your retirement,
and success in whatever you do. I hope that I will see you
again from time to time.

Thank you again,

Robin

Robin Easey

This letter from Robin is appreciated more than anyone can imagine.
These were tough times for us all but we shall never forget you and
your family for the sacrifice you made for the City of Nepean. We are
indebted to you forever.

Thanks.

Ewart Gus Wersch, Chief of Police, Nepean

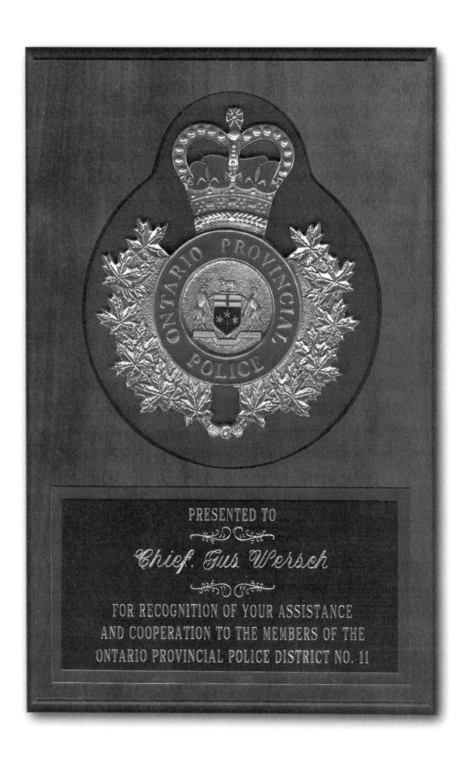

PRESENTED TO

Chief Gus Wersch

FOR RECOGNITION OF YOUR ASSISTANCE
AND COOPERATION TO THE MEMBERS OF THE
ONTARIO PROVINCIAL POLICE DISTRICT NO. 11

Gwen and Bert Easey were involved at many functions appearing as a duet and strumming their guitars. Staff Sergeant Bert Easey is the father of Constable Robin Easey injured at the Bayshore Shopping Centre in 1984. Thanks for your dedicated service to the Nepean Police and the City of Nepean.

CANADA

THE HONOURABLE / L'HONORABLE
CHARLES F. DOYLE
JUDGE / JUGE
DISTRICT COURT OF ONTARIO
COUR DE DISTRICT DE L'ONTARIO

JUDGE'S CHAMBERS / CABINET DU JUGE
COURT HOUSE / PALAIS DE JUSTICE
161 ELGIN STREET / 161, RUE ELGIN
OTTAWA, ONTARIO
K2P 2K1

June 3rd, 1988.

Chief E.G. Wersch,
68 Avonlea Road,
Nepean, Ontario.
K2G 0J5

Dear Gus:

I regret very much that I shall be unable to attend the Testimonial Dinner/Dance in your honour next Friday.

As senior judge in Eastern Ontario, (District #6), I am co-host of our annual district meeting to be held beginning Thursday, June 9th, 1988 and continuing until Saturday, June 11th, 1988. It is to be presided over by Chief Judge Lyon and is being held out of town.

I must say that I thoroughly enjoyed and appreciated the co-operation and friendship you showed me when I was a member of the Nepean Police Commission. Your dedication to your post was obvious and the recognition of your past efficient service is well-deserved.

Please accept the very best wishes of Frances and myself in your new undertaking and for many happy years of retirement (?).

Sincerely,

Charles F. Doyle

Embassy of the United States of America

Office of the Legal Attache
100 Wellington Street
Ottawa, Ontario K1P 5T1

June 6, 1988

Chief Gus Wersch
Nepean Police Force
245 Greenbank Road
Nepean, Ontario K2H 8W9

Dear Chief Wersch:

My colleagues in the Federal Bureau of Investigation join me in extending congratulations on your retirement after a long and distinguished career in law enforcement.

The citizens of Nepean will miss your professionalism and dedication. Your perception in recruiting bright young officers to the Nepean Police Force is a legacy you can be proud of.

I wish you success and happiness as you begin a new phase of your life.

Sincerely yours,

John E. Keary-Taylor
Legal Attache

POLICE BADGES
1957-1982

Police Badges and Shoulder Flashes, 1957-1982

Special thanks to all the civilian staff that have served in the various departments, branches as secretaries, clerical and stenographer duties in support of the police service.

A special thanks to the ladies who took me (Chief Gus Wersch) out for a farewell luncheon as shown in the photograph above. As a special remembrance of note, during the years that the above staff worked in the various offices, I had a habit of walking around to see how things were going. I always had a pocket full of candies and when I stopped at the various desks I would give the staff a candy to cheer them up before the end of their shift. With 27 of the clerical staff attending my luncheon, they apparently decided to present me with a large basket of candies – 27 pounds. This wasn't just a return of the candies but to make a statement that the thoughtfulness had been appreciated.

Your thoughtfulness and generosity are a memorable highlight in my career.

SO LONG CHIEF GUS WERSCH

This is the story of Chief Gus Wersch
Although many a time he was called a lot worse
He came to Nepean as Sergeant in 64
Was a Cop with O.P.P. the 8 years before.

There were only 20 men, a fairly small force,
In April 66, for Chief he was Aubrey's choice.
Claimed he was going to get things on track
But some days the O.P.P. almost got him back.

***

"Behind every good man stands a woman"
Is an addage we've heard many times before
But truth be told; any good boss
Has a great secretary just outside the door.

So it seems only fair at this glorious event
That I should come forth and take score
Of all the great accomplishments
That I have allowed him to take credit for.

It has been twelve long years in the prime of my life
I've devoted to this town
Keeping him stocked with cookies and glitter mints
An empty candy jar would always make him frown.

He speaks sometimes of when he was hired
Politicians expressed reservations
Hopefully now they have all changed their minds
If accomplishments are a fair indication.

His basic approach right from the start
For this community to Ottawa's west
Was to build a small Force that did a good job
And was recognized as one of the best.

We hear of accolades far and wide
Of how Nepean's become so great
Gus must have seen it coming
Cause he has made his police force first rate.

School patrols and open neck shirts
Were a couple of his firsts
Drop down holsters, propane vehicles,
The implementation of roadside alerts.

Firearms training, preventive intervention
Distinctively marked patrol cars
A police library, employee assistance
Front line officers trained in C.P.R.

These are merely a sampling of what...
He's initiated for Nepean to see
That with honest effort and innovation
How good our police force could be.

The best of luck to Gus and Fran
He will finally have time to spend with his wife.
He has after all given twenty-four years
To protecting Nepean's quality of life.

***

It sure will be different without him.
As a boss he was always the best.
He treated me well, and I thank him
And I know he'll delight in some rest.

Rosemarie Albert
June 10, 1988

Speech by Rose Marie Albert, Secretary to the Chief of Police as a farewell tribute.

After my retirement on May 31st, 1988, I received a telephone call from Councillor Margaret Rywak that a street in the Stonebridge Development had been named "Wersch Lane" to recognize my years of service in Nepean.

Above photos: Rose Marie Albert after making presentation and Chief Ewart Gus Wersch thanking all in attendance for their presence. June 10ᵗʰ, 1988.

THIS SONG IS TO BE SUNG TO THE SONG "MY WAY"

And now it's time to go
To say good-bye
To sing your praises
You did what you had to do
You started out oh so certain
In 49 an O.P.P.
You travelled each and every highway
But more much more than this
You did it your way.

In 64 the time had come
You made a move to Nepean
Within a two year span
You reached your peak
Without exemption
And as the years went by
We got our new police centre
Our thanks we give to you
You did it your way.

REFRAIN   Oh what is a Chief
What has he got
If not his pride
Than he is not
The E.G. WERSCH we've come to know
As he has helped Nepean grow
You've made us proud
And we stand tall
You did it your way.

Changes there's been alot
To which we are so very grateful
Computers were introduced
And our records automated
To think you did all that
And so much more we will remember
And more much more than this
You did it your way

REFRAIN   Oh what is a Chief
What has he got
If not his pride
Than he is not
The E.G. WERSCH we've come to know
As he has helped Nepean grow
You've made us proud
And we stand tall
You did it your way

You've made us proud and we stand tall
You did it your way.

Ken & Wanda LOGAN
04Apr88

Sung by Cornwall Police Band

Toast to the Pipers for a job well done at the retirement dinner:
Cst. L. Bisaillion of Nepean and Chief Neil Raven of Deep River, Ontario.

Frances Wersch and Chief Gus Wersch at head table, June 10th, 1988.

Farewell...

*Chief Neill Raven, Deep River, and Piper Cst. L. Bisaillion, Nepean Police.
Farewell Salute to Chief Gus Wersch, June 10th, 1988*

General Observation and Message

I hear many so called arm chair critics who have all the answers after the fact. They have weeks or even months to discuss the action taken but when officers have to take and make split second decisions, there is no time for second guessing. They do not have the luxury of time on their hands, as demonstrated by these two cases – David Utman who died and Robin Easey and Ralph Erfle who were seriously injured.

There are no great men or women, there are only challenges that ordinary men or women are forced by circumstances to meet. Police officers meet and face these challenges daily without notice.

Progress is not without its "errors or omissions" – it's part of the learning curve. The Nepean police officers have been involved in many community events and initiated many fund-raising events for charitable purposes which has helped to bond that trust and friendship that is so necessary to have an open dialogue with the residents of the community. "We were never the untouchables."

When we started in 1964 it seemed like a long journey. Many things were accomplished, and we certainly changed the police service from those early years.

There are many stories to tell, the few inclusions herein are an attempt to cover the broad spectrum of my personal involvement and that of members of the police service throughout this period of time.

On looking back, it seems but a moment in time. As the Officers reach their retirement age, they can look back and know that they have proven themselves by example and dedication to the job. We all have left our footprints in the sands of time!

The Final Page in the Nepean Police Service 1988-1994

The history of the Nepean Police Service has been documented from records and personal involvement from 1964-1988 until my retirement on May 31st, 1988.

One of my efforts was to create an on going history of the Nepean Police. This was accomplished by publishing an Annual Report starting in 1965 and ending in 1987. Copies of these years have been retained. Occurrence books with newspaper clippings were saved from 1964 to 1988. Photographs of the Nepean Police involvements were saved and were available in the production of this history.

These items proved to be invaluable and will be made available to the Nepean Museum to produce a first class presentation of the Nepean Police Service. The Nepean Police Officers played a major role in the development of the history of the City of Nepean.

Deputy Chief Wayne Phillips was promoted to Chief of Police of Nepean effective June 1st, 1988.

The City of Nepean Police Service was amalgamated, along with all of the Carleton County area by the City of Ottawa, effective January 1st, 1994.

This officially ended my police service in Carleton County and Nepean in particular.

In closing I wish to take this opportunity to thank all the officers and the civilian support staff for your loyal and dedicated service. Your presence has made the City of Nepean a better place to live and I wish you well as you continue your journey in the police service, or other vocations of your choice.

Thanks for the privilege. To the Staff and Citizens of Nepean.

Acknowledgments:

Staff Sgt. Ron Driscoll for his input in this history report, and to Staff Sgt. Brian McGarvey and Sgt. Wayne Levere for the police activity photographs used in this report. The officers and staff of the Identification Branch for their assistance, and all the police officers and civilian staff who made it possible to provide the police service above and beyond the call of duty in exemplary manner.

[signature]

Ewart Gus Wersch, Chief of Police, Retired. May 31st, 1988

About the Author

Gus Wersch with his best friend

It's been a long journey, but as I look back it seems but a moment in time.

I started out in life in central Manitoba, in a farming community near a town called Moosehorn 120 miles North of Winnipeg. I was born on March 15th, 1927 and raised on a farm with my parents, two older brothers and a younger sister. We were introduced to the hardships of life in the depression years of the 1930's.

This early experience in life developed our strengths to survive in those difficult times. Our parents provided us with guidance and insisted that we obtain a high school education as most children in the area seemed to drop out of school at grade eight level.

We were lucky in a way, that by living on the farm we had the best of produce, but other things like hydro, motor vehicles and a farm tractor were too costly so everything had to be done by hand and with the use of horse power.

The money from the sale of farm goods was limited, so we improvised. Our mother was an excellent cook and seamstress and this improved our daily living. As an example she would buy the empty hundred pound canvas sugar and cloth flour bags for five cents each from the local general store. These were dyed different colors and with her skills on the manual Singer sewing machine she made us jeans and jackets to wear to school and they looked like regular factory bought clothes.

Our transportation was with horses which were also used for cultivation of fields.

At age the age of five years we would start going to school in Moosehorn two miles from home. We walked most of the time which in winter was difficult. Roads were not plowed as very few cars were in the neighborhood. School buses were non-existent.

All the students in the Manitoba schools recieved a certificate commemorating the visit by their Majesties King George the Vl and Queen Elizabeth (Mother of present Queen) to Canada in 1939. We chershed this memento and preserved it to this day.

In 1940 the measles struck our area as everywhere else. Most of the children were sick, but we suffered extremely hard as my oldest brother passed away from the effects of the measles at the age of 17. This was a difficult time for our family.

On graduation from high school in the spring of 1944 the Manitoba Department of Education representative came to our high school and offered the graduates a 3 month Teachers Training Course at the Wesley United College in Winnipeg from mid June to September. I attended this course and on completion I was assigned to The Marne Public School, a one room country school. In the 1944-45 school year, I taught 29 children from beginners to grade eight. The oldest pupil was 15 and I, as the teacher, was 17 years old.

This experience led me to follow my ambitions to become a police officer, but I had to wait until I was age 21 to apply, so I left for the Red Lake Ontario gold mines. Until the fall of 1949 I worked in the mines and when I was transferred to Toronto, Ontario in late September of 1949 at the age of 22 years, I applied to the Ontario Provincial Police and was accepted as a recruit.

All the recruits were sent to the Ontario Provincial Police College at Ajax, Ontario on an intensive training course from November 1st to December 19th, 1949. On graduation we were sent to our postings to the various detachments in Ontario.

My posting was to No. 11 District, Cornwall, and on to the Ottawa detachment located at 1663 Bank Street, Ottawa, arriving on December 20th 1949 to start my police career. I met Sergeant John Hinchliffe, officer in charge and the two Corporals, Carl Johns and George Nault along with four Constables, and with my arrival we increased our police strength to eight officers to Police Carleton County, which included ten townships (including the Township of Nepean). On December 21st, 1949 I was assigned to Car 1129 and dropped off at the Manotick Tea Room where my room and board had been arranged. My area of patrol and answering all police calls for service included four Townships – Nepean, North Gower, Marlborough and Goulbourn.

This was the official beginning of my police career. I worked six days per week, covering a period of twelve hours per day, was on call after hours and on Sundays. I worked in this area and traveled to the Ottawa detachment to complete reports, attend meetings, etc.

In the fall of 1953 I was transferred to work full time from the Ottawa office on Criminal Investigations for the whole of Carleton County until January 12th, 1964 when I left the Ontario Provincial Police and joined the newly established Township of Nepean Police as Sergeant in charge of Operations.

The Chief of Police for the Township of Nepean was John Rankin, who came to Nepean from the joint Gloucester-Nepean Police which had been established in 1957 and dissolved on December 31st, 1963.

After two short years Chief John Rankin suffered a serious illness and passed away in March 1966. The Nepean Police Commissioners of the day appointed me as the Chief of Police for Nepean Township effective April 1st, 1966 until my retirement on May 31st, 1988.

The police service provided me with the opportunity to serve the residents of Carleton County in general and Nepean in particular for more than 38 years.

Retirement

Since my retirement I continued to live in Nepean and always felt that the police history of Carleton County should be made available to residents and beyond. Nepean Township dates back to the early days when its area was part of the west and northern part of Ottawa, which had the name derived from Sir Evan Nepean of historical interest.

Yes, its been a long journey and there are many stories to tell involving the changes that have taken place over the years.

It has been my desire to put the history of policing in Carleton County and Nepean in particular together covering the period from 1909 when the Provincial Police of Ontario was established with the many changes along the way, until my retirement in 1988.

In 1994 Ottawa amalgamated the police service extending the Ottawa Police Service to cover all of Carleton County.

Nepean Museum

All my police service items, such as my O.P.P. and Nepean Police uniforms and related items have been donated to the Nepean Museum along with photographs and written material that was part of the development of the police service in Carleton County.

The Nepean Museum staff are to be commended for the excellent presentation of the police items supplied as support to this history. The Museum Project opened on November 2nd, 2008 and is available for public viewing.

Publishing of Contents

The history of the Ontario Provincial Police from its establishment in 1909 to 1949 in general as presented was authorized by written permission to be used as part of this publication.

This project is too important not to be completed as it is a major part of the development of this area. A special thanks and appreciation goes out to all the staff of the Nepean Police Service for their support. Without your dedicated service, this history would not be possible.

Ewart Gus Wersch, Chief of Police Retired.